INFORMIX-OnLine

Performance

Tuning

Elizabeth Suto

PRENTICE HALL PTR, UPPER SADDLE RIVER, NJ 07458

Library of Congress Cataloging-in-Publication Data

Suto, Elizabeth.
    Informix-online performance tuning / Elizabeth Suto.
        p.   cm.
    Includes index.
    ISBN 0-13-124322-5
    1. Databases management   2. INFORMIX-OnLine   3. Client/server
computing   I. Title
    QA76.9.D3S9415   1995   94-35128
    05.75'65 -- dc20   CIP

© 1995 by Prentice Hall PTR
Prentice-Hall, Inc.
A Simon & Schuster Co.
Upper Saddle River, New Jersey 07458

▮▮ INFORMIX®*Press*

Informix Press
Informix© Software, Inc.
4100 Bohannon Drive
Menlo Park, CA 94025

Cover design director: *Jerry Votta*
Cover design: *Karen Marsilio*
Acquisitions editor: *Mark L. Taub*
Editorial assistant: *Marcy Levine*
Production Editor: *Camille Trentacoste*

Manager, Informix Press: *Todd Katz*
Founder, Informix Press: *Suzanne Fuery*

The publisher offers discounts on this book when ordered in bulk quantities.
For more information, contact:

> Corporate Sales Department, PTR Prentice Hall, 113 Sylvan Avenue, Englewood Cliffs, NJ 07632
> Phone: 800-382-3419, Fax: 201-592-2249, E-mail: dan_rush@prenhall.com

The following are worldwide trademarks of Informix Software, Inc., or its subsidiaries, registered in the United States as indicated by "®," and in numerous other countries worldwide: INFORMIX-OnLine®, INFORMIX-SE®, and INFORMIX-SQL.®

All other brands and product names in this publication are registered trademarks or trademarks of their respective holders.

Printed in the United States of America

10 9 8 7 6 5 4 3

ISBN 0-13-124322-5

Prentice-Hall International (UK) Limited, *London*
Prentice-Hall of Australia Pty. Limited, *Sydney*
Prentice-Hall Canada Inc., *Toronto*
Prentice-Hall Hispanoamericana, S.A., *Mexico*
Prentice-Hall of India Private Limited, *New Delhi*
Prentice-Hall of Japan, Inc., *Tokyo*
Simon & Schuster Asia Pte. Ltd., *Singapore*
Editora Prentice-Hall do Brasil, Ltda., *Rio de Janeiro*

Contents

Chapter 1

Introduction to INFORMIX-OnLine

The purpose of this chapter is to give new administrators the minimum amount of information necessary to understand the rest of the chapters in this book. The INFORMIX-OnLine database server is somewhat complex and carries its own terminology. However, with a basic knowledge, you can perform basic monitoring and tuning tasks.

In 1993, Informix released version 6.0 of INFORMIX-OnLine Dynamic Server, which contains significant architectural changes. Shortly after, version 7.0 of INFORMIX-OnLine Dynamic Server was released with a few more performance features. This chapter will discuss the architecture and terminology of both the 5.0 version and the 6.0 version. The additional features of version 7.0 are explained in a later chapter.

The distinctions between INFORMIX-OnLine and INFORMIX-OnLine Dynamic Server are pointed out in all chapters of the book. Both versions are referred to as "OnLine" for simplicity.

The topics covered in this chapter are:

- Overview of the INFORMIX-OnLine and INFORMIX-OnLine Dynamic Server architectures
- Processing an SQL statement
- Checkpoints and logging
- Client/server communication
- Multiple OnLine systems

1.1 OVERVIEW OF THE ONLINE ARCHITECTURE

OnLine is a database server, which means that it acts as a liaison between a user and a database. INFORMIX-OnLine is responsible for reading and writing data to and from the

1

database, controlling and optimizing access to the database, and protecting and preserving the integrity of the data.

Disk, memory, and processes together make up what is known as the *OnLine system* or *database server*, although it is actually the processes within the system that are doing the work.

INFORMIX-OnLine Process Architecture (Version 5.0)

INFORMIX-OnLine 5.0 is based on a two-process model. The first process, the client application, is responsible for all interaction with the user via a user interface. When an application encounters an SQL statement, it passes that statement to the second process, the database server, via the UNIX Inter-Process Communication (IPC) pipes mechanism. The database server (the process name is **sqlturbo**) is responsible for parsing, optimizing and executing the SQL statement, retrieving any requested data, and passing the data back to the application (see Figure 1.1).

Figure 1.1-   The 5.0 database server process architecture

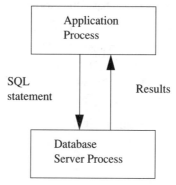

For every user there are two processes. The application process can run on the same machine as the database server process, or on another "client" machine. Although this architecture is very good with fewer users, with hundreds of users, the large number of processes consumes the operating system, which has to handle context switching between all the processes.

INFORMIX-OnLine Dynamic Server Process Architecture (Version 6.0)

INFORMIX-OnLine Dynamic Server (Version 6.0) is fundamentally different from previous versions because it uses a multithreaded architecture (see Figure 1.2). In this version, fewer processes can handle the workload of hundreds, even thousands of users.

These database server processes are called *virtual processors*, or *vps*. A vp belongs to a *vp class*, which has a responsibility for a set of tasks. For example, the AIO (Asynchronous I/O) vps are responsible for all nonlogging I/O. The CPU vps handle most of the CPU-intensive work.

The virtual processors are normal UNIX processes—these processes make up the database server, or the OnLine system.

Figure 1.2-   The 6.0 database server process architecture

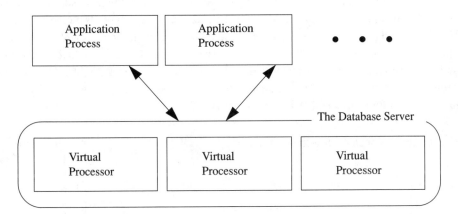

A *thread* is an entity in a virtual processor that has its own context, meaning its own pointer to a place in the code (program counter) and its own data variables. At any one time, only one thread within the process is running, while the others must wait. A multi-threaded process cuts down on the operating system overhead, as UNIX only sees and administers one process. You can think of a thread as "taking over" the process when it runs. When the thread completes its work, the thread lets another thread "take over" the process. In this way, one process is running on behalf of more than one user. All the multi-threading activities are internal to the Informix database server.

Each application process connecting to the database server is known as a *session*. The session has one or more threads associated with it. The threads are responsible for executing the SQL statements requested by the application.

A session thread runs on vps in the CPU vp class. It can migrate across any CPU vp, which keeps a vp from getting tied up with a single thread. All CPU vps take threads that are ready to run from the same ready queue.

When a session thread must wait for any reason (such as for a lock or disk I/O), it performs a *context switch*, which means it yields control of the process to another thread waiting to run in the ready queue. It will put itself on the wait or sleep queue while waiting for the resource. Another vp, called the AIO (Asynchronous I/O) vp will normally perform the I/O on behalf of the session and wake up the waiting session thread when the I/O has completed.

Note that a thread context switch is similar to a UNIX process context switch, except that less data needs to be swapped for a thread context switch. Also, the thread context switch is completely transparent to the operating system.

Figure 1.3 shows an example of a thread context switch. Thread 6 is currently running on the virtual processor. Thread 6 requires some data that is on disk, so it must yield the CPU virtual processor while it waits for the disk I/O. Thread 6 sends a read request to the AIO vp and puts its context on a sleep queue (step 1). Next, thread 6 replaces its context with the context of the next thread in the ready queue, thread 33 (step 2). Once this happens, thread 33 effectively controls the CPU virtual processor. When the AIO vp performs the disk read for thread 6, thread 6 is moved from the sleep queue to the ready queue, to wait for an available CPU vp to run (step 3).

Figure 1.3-   Thread context switch

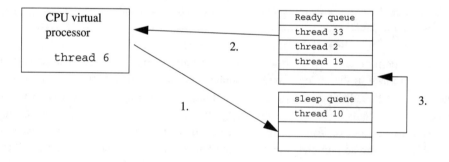

In addition to the CPU vp and the AIO vp, there are several other vp classes:

- LIO vps—The LIO vps write transaction log records to the logical log on disk. One LIO vp is automatically started. Two will be started if the disk that has the logical log is mirrored.

- PIO vps—The PIO vps write log records to the physical log on disk. One PIO vp is automatically started. Two will be started if the disk that has the physical log is mirrored.

- ADM vp—One ADM vp is started as a timer and is responsible for waking up threads that are sleeping for a certain period of time.

• Network vps (SHM, SOC, TLI)—These vps are usually responsible for polling for requests from client applications. The number and type of network vps are configurable by the administrator.

1.2   DISK TERMINOLOGY

OnLine handles its own disk management. You allocate a set of files or raw device space, and OnLine will allocate databases and tables in that space, along with control information and log space. Figure 1.4 gives an example of the components of OnLine disk storage.

You add space to OnLine in large contiguous blocks called *chunks*. Chunks can range from one megabyte to two gigabytes in size. A chunk can be a part of a disk or the entire disk. Chunks are allocated in a logical grouping called a *dbspace*. A dbspace represents one or more chunks that are used for a similar purpose. For example, you can place a table in a dbspace, and the rows will be placed in any chunk that is a part of that dbspace.

Chunks are subdivided into *pages*. A page is a fixed contiguous unit of space, usually either 2 kbytes or 4 kbytes in size, depending upon the hardware and operating system you are using. Pages are created to hold certain kinds of information, such as data or indexes. An index does not coexist with the data on the same page.

Figure 1.4-   Pages, chunks, dbspaces and extents

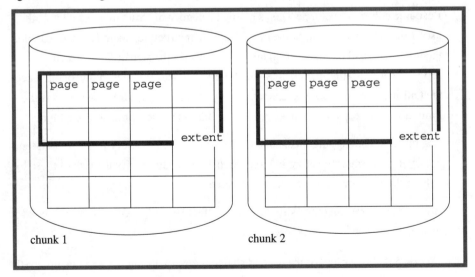

dbspace 1

When a table is created, it is assigned a set of pages to use. Each "set" is physically contiguous within a chunk and is called an *extent*. When these pages fill with data, another extent is allocated on the same or different chunk within the dbspace. Extents are used to group pages from the same table together on a chunk that might contain data and index pages from more than one table.

The extent sizes for each table can be specified with the CREATE TABLE and ALTER TABLE statements. The collection of extents for a table is sometimes referred to as a *tblspace*. Each tblspace has an internal identification number associated with it, called a *tblspace number*.

1.3   SHARED MEMORY

Shared memory is used to hold data structures used frequently by the OnLine system. Some of the shared memory structures common to both the 5.0 and 6.0 versions are:

- The buffer cache. This is usually a substantial area in shared memory where pages on disk are temporarily held. By using pages in memory rather than on disk, you can decrease the number of disk reads and writes that occur. Since the buffer pool is shared by all users, one user can take advantage of a page brought into the buffer pool by another user without performing a disk read.

- Resource control structures. This is a broad category of structures that control the use of the OnLine system. Some of the important structures include the lock table, the user table, and the transaction table. You specify the size of these structures by a series of configuration parameters which will be discussed later in this book. Once the OnLine system is up, you cannot modify the size of the structures. This is the limitation that keeps the number of locks and users at their predetermined limit.

- Log buffers. The logging mechanism uses some shared memory pages to hold temporary log information before it is sent to disk. You can specify the size of these log buffers through several configuration parameters.

How these shared memory structures can affect performance will be discussed in later chapters.

Version 5.0 allocates all of the needed shared memory during the initialization of the OnLine instance. Figure 1.5 shows shared memory in version 5.0.

Figure 1.5-   Shared memory in version 5.0

Lock table	User table	Chunk table	Logical log buffer
Latch table	Transaction table	Dbspace table	Physical log buffer
Buffer cache			

Shared Memory in 6.0

In the 6.0 version of OnLine, the amount of shared memory needed by the OnLine system increases dramatically. This is because the memory normally used by the individual **sqlturbo** processes in version 5.0 is implemented in shared memory in version 6.0. The 6.0 shared memory is divided into three separate sets of segments:

- The *resident* segments. These segments hold the same information that was found in version 5.0—mainly the buffer cache and various shared memory structures.

- The *virtual* segments. These segments hold all the information needed in order to run the threads, such as the thread context. Also, any other memory needed to cache stored procedures or perform a sort is also allocated here. Virtual segments are added as needed while the OnLine system is running.

- The *message* segments. These segments hold messages used in communicating with the application by shared memory Inter-Process Communication (IPC).

1.4   PROCESSING AN SQL STATEMENT

The client application process passes the SQL statement (e.g., INSERT, UPDATE, DELETE, or SELECT) to the database server, which is responsible for parsing, optimizing, and executing the statement, and returning the resulting data.

Usually, during the course of executing the statement, data must be read from the database. The database server determines the pages that need to be read to satisfy the SQL statement. If the needed page is in the shared memory buffer cache, it will be read from memory. If not, the page is read from disk and put in the shared memory buffer cache. Since the buffer cache is shared, other users can access the same page in memory without having to perform a disk read. The more often data is read from memory and not disk, the higher the *read cache rate*. Systems with a high read cache rate are obviously more efficient.

When the SQL statement requires a write to the database (INSERT, UPDATE, or DELETE), the database server will write to the page in the buffer cache. When a page is written in memory, it is marked as *dirty*, meaning it must eventually be copied to disk. The write to disk is put off as long as possible, in hopes that multiple users write to the same page in memory, or a single user writes to the same page in memory multiple times. The more often the same page is written in memory, the higher the *write cache rate*. Systems with a high write cache rate are more efficient.

1.5   CHECKPOINTS AND LOGICAL AND PHYSICAL LOGGING

The buffer cache is an important component of the OnLine system, as it decreases the amount of disk reads and writes that are necessary in SQL operations. However, by writing to memory rather than disk, we are in danger of losing data that has not yet been committed to disk. OnLine uses three mechanisms to prevent the loss of data: *checkpoints*, *logical logs*, and *physical logs*.

Before writing to a page in memory, the OnLine system does two things:

1.   It takes a before-image of that page (a copy of the page before it was changed) and writes it to the physical log buffer, which is another area in shared memory. When the physical log buffer is full, it is flushed to an area on disk called the physical log.

2.   It writes a record of the change in the logical log buffer in shared memory. When this buffer is full, it is flushed to an area on disk called the logical log. The logical log buffer could actually be flushed to disk more often if a special kind of logging called "unbuffered logging" is used. Unbuffered logging will be discussed in a later chapter.

Figure 1.6 shows the steps of writing data to disk.

Figure 1.6-   Steps taken to write data to disk

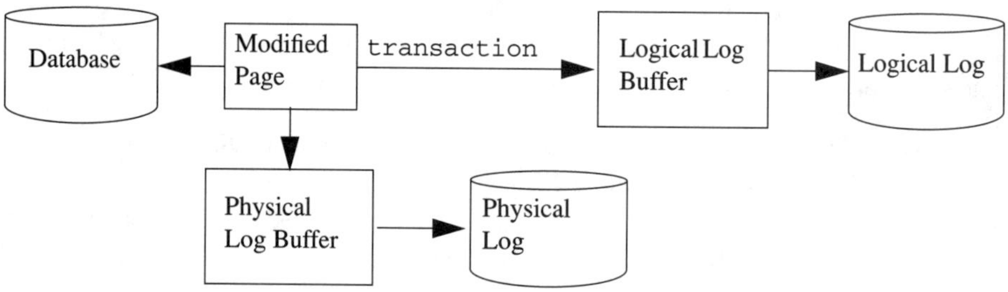

Every few minutes (the actual amount of time is configurable), the OnLine system forces a checkpoint to occur. A checkpoint is the synchronization of data that is on disk with data that is in memory. The OnLine system synchronizes data by doing the following:

1.   Any pages in the physical log buffer are flushed to disk.

2.   All pages that have been modified in memory (*dirty pages*) are written to disk.

3.   An entry is made in the logical log marking the time the checkpoint occurred.

4.   The physical log file is cleared. The physical log stores pages that have been changed between checkpoints. These pages are no longer necessary once the checkpoint completes.

5.   The logical log buffer is flushed to disk.

The logical log, the physical log, and the checkpoint are all used for recovery. Suppose the OnLine system goes down during a heavy period of activity. Since data in memory has most certainly been altered, OnLine must recover to a point where all incomplete transactions are rolled back. To do this, OnLine must do the following:

1.   All the pages in the physical log file are written to disk. After this step, OnLine has effectively restored the OnLine system to the time of the last checkpoint.

2.   All the logical log entries put on disk since the last checkpoint are applied. After this step, OnLine will be restored to the last time the logical log buffer was flushed to disk from the log buffer in shared memory.

3.   OnLine uses the logical log to roll back all uncompleted transactions; that is, transactions that have no logical log entry to COMMIT WORK.

A set of processes (threads in version 6.0) called page cleaners are responsible for writing modified pages to disk. They write pages to disk either during a checkpoint or, if the buffer cache gets too "dirty," between checkpoints.

1.6   CLIENT/SERVER COMMUNICATION

5.0 Local Communication

In version 5.0, when the application process and the database server are on the same machine, they communicate to each other via the UNIX inter-process communication (IPC) mechanism of unnamed pipes. Pipes are an efficient method of communication between two processes.

6.0 Local Communication

In version 6.0, since the two-process architecture is replaced with the multithreaded architecture, the methods of local communication have changed. You can use either shared memory or TCP/IP as a communication mechanism between the application process and the database server.

The shared-memory method uses the message segments in shared memory to hold messages sent back and forth from the application and the database server.

TCP/IP uses the TCP/IP protocol to send and receive messages. When the communication is between processes on the same machine, a method of communication called *local loopback* is used. On most machines, this means that the processes do not actually go out across the network to deliver the messages, since the client and server are both on the same machine.

The 6.0 application uses an environment variable, called INFORMIXSERVER, to determine how to connect to an OnLine system. INFORMIXSERVER is a key into a file called the **sqlhosts** file, which gives more information on how to connect to the OnLine system:

- The host name where the OnLine system is running

- The type of communication (TCP/IP or shared memory)

- The port number, if TCP/IP is used

The sqlhosts file is in the directory $INFORMIXDIR/etc. For more information about the format of this file, consult your Informix documentation.

Remote Communication

TCP/IP using the TLI or Sockets programming interface is usually used to perform client/server communication when the application and the database server reside on different machines.

In version 5.0, the application cannot communicate directly to the database server across the network. Instead, the communication occurs through an intermediate database server on the client side (see Figure 1.7). This process is either a relay module (which can be used with release 5.0 applications) or an actual database server that only performs communication tasks.

For version 6.0 applications, the communication libraries are embedded in the application code, so no additional process is needed on the client system (see Figure 1.8).

Figure 1.7- Remote client server communication in 5.0

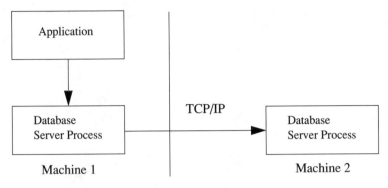

Figure 1.8- Remote client server communication in 6.0

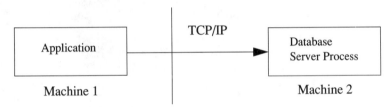

1.7 MULTIPLE ONLINE SYSTEMS

It is possible to have more than one OnLine system on one machine. Each OnLine system is sometimes known as an OnLine instance. An OnLine instance has its own processes, shared memory, and disk. OnLine instances cannot communicate in any way except through the remote client/server communication method, TCP/IP. The shared memory is kept separate by using a different shared memory key.

1.8 FOR MORE INFORMATION...

If you are interested in more information about the internal architecture of the OnLine system, refer to the product documentation, *INFORMIX-OnLine Administrator's Guide.*

Chapter 2

Performance Tuning

The world of performance analysis starts in one place: defining the problem to be solved or decision to be made. Tuning configuration parameters or changing database design means nothing unless an issue can be solved by doing it.

This chapter will cover the following topics:

- Proactive vs. reactive performance considerations
- Determining performance expectations
- How to approach performance issues
- Performance tests
- Performance tools and monitors
- Configuration parameters

2.1   PROACTIVE VS. REACTIVE PERFORMANCE CONSIDERATIONS

Performance issues can be divided into two types, *proactive* and *reactive*.

Proactive performance issues are those that affect future decisions of an organization. They should surface while planning for a new or revised production environment. They are easier to define and easier to measure. In addition, by pinpointing potential problems during the planning phase, you can set the expectations of management and users of the kind of performance they will experience during a production environment, and you can avoid some of the reactive performance issues that may occur once a system is in place.

Some possible proactive performance issues might be:

- Evaluate database design alternatives
- Evaluate data distribution options

- Check program designs

- Compare distributed database performance versus nondistributed database performance

- Compare client/server performance versus single-system performance

- Evaluate whether the hardware is sufficient to support possible production database activity

- Determine expected response times in average queries

- Determine how growth in the size of a table will affect the overall query performance

Reactive performance issues are usually those that occur once a system is in production, such as:

- Complaints from users about response time

- Unexpectedly lengthy completion time of certain activities (reports, index builds, massive data loads, etc.)

- Inability to perform tasks in a specific period of time, such as archives, data loads, and so on

Once a reactive performance issue occurs, the cause can be one of a myriad of different possibilities. Also, the amount of time an administrator has to solve a reactive performance issue is usually much less than if problems were found during the design or production planning phase.

2.9   DETERMINING PERFORMANCE EXPECTATIONS

End users usually perceive performance in terms of *response time*. Response time is usually defined as the interval of time between when the user presses the Execute or Return key on the workstation or terminal and when the information is returned and displayed on the screen.

It is important to determine an acceptable response time for each critical activity and even more important to make sure the performance criteria are written down and agreed to by all parties involved in an application development project.

A common mistake in development projects is to either ignore performance issues altogether in the design document or state performance goals in a vague manner. Here's an example of a vague response-time goal:

"All users should get a response back within 3 seconds."

In addition to being unrealistic, this goal is also vague. Do all parties understand what response time is? A three-second response time severely restricts the application developer to keeping *all* transactions very small in order to meet the response-time goal.

Here's an example of a response-time goal that is a little more realistic and more specific to the application:

> "When a user presses the Execute key in any screen in the reservation application, the database transaction should be completed and a response returned to the user within 3 seconds 80% of the time, and within 6 seconds 20% of the time."

The goal states the application where it is applicable. Some applications can be organized in groups of like database activity, such as table maintenance screens, and can be given the same performance goal. In addition, the goal allows for some slippage during busy periods. A highly utilized disk or processor can severely affect response time.

Another type of measurement that might be important in a system is *throughput*, where a certain amount of activity must be accomplished in a fixed amount of time. This measurement is most important during batch activities, such as reporting, data loading, and so on. The system design document should address these requirements as well, for example:

> "The mainframe transfer application runs nightly and must load 32,000 rows in the transaction table, and 10,000 rows in the contact table. This activity must complete in 5 hours."

Once the performance goals are stated in writing, it is the administrator's responsibility that those goals be met. Unless you like the idea of telling the application development staff that an application redesign is necessary, or putting in a purchase order for last-minute hardware, *don't wait until the last minute to test out these performance goals in a benchmark environment*!

2.10 HOW TO APPROACH PERFORMANCE ISSUES

1. Define what unit of work you will measure. For example, you may be testing the ability of the hardware to handle 50 users running a certain type of transaction and still maintaining the response time specified in the performance goals.

2. Determine how you will measure it. For proper measurement of improvements, you must have two things:

   • A repeatable test. Without a repeatable test, there is no way to accurately measure improvements. However, it is just this factor that is missing in most reactive performance situations. Whatever the reason (lack of a proper test environment, lack of time for a proper test, lack of statistics), many times an administrator is forced to make adjustments in tunable parameters and rely solely on the word of a user to judge whether a change was effective. Although measuring activity in the ever-changing production environment is not the best method, sometimes it is the only choice. Thankfully, there are tools that come with the operating system and with OnLine that can be used to determine the effectiveness of many types of parameter changes in the absence of a repeatable test.

- A reliable measure of true activity. When choosing a measurement, make sure it approximates true production activity. This means you will have to reproduce at least a subset of the production system in a test environment. For example, to test response time in a production environment with 50 users, it would be inappropriate to measure response time in a test environment with five users. Although you can attempt to model a larger user population given the results of a small number of users, this technique is risky because of the large number of performance variables that can interfere with performance.

3.   Determine the factors that affect the performance issue you are studying. This step is where your knowledge of OnLine, the operating system, and the hardware is most important. This step is what the rest of this book is about. You must understand the relationships that the OnLine configuration parameters have with each other and with the rest of the system.

4.   Perform tests. This is where the actual analysis work occurs. It is important here to proceed like you did in school science projects—with a careful and impartial test, and good recording of the results. Make sure the test interval is long enough to eliminate the effect of start-up and completion activities. In addition, it is very important to confine the number of variables between tests to one. For example, if you run a test, change several parameters and rerun the test with better results, which parameter actually helped performance? Ideally, the discipline you should follow is shown in Figure 2.1.

Figure 2.1-   The test execution cycle.

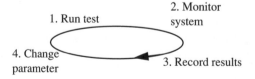

5.   Evaluate performance. This step is where you prepare the test results you gathered in the previous step and determine which factors improved or hampered perfor-

mance. If you are preparing results for management, you must place your conclusions in a well-prepared document.

2.11 PERFORMANCE TESTS: STANDARD TESTS OR CUSTOM TESTS

It is not unusual to spend several weeks writing a test to approximate your production activity, especially in the early stages of a project. Because of the extra time required to write custom tests, some administrators and system evaluators choose to rely on standard tests to approximate performance. The most common tests for evaluating database performance are those specified by the Transaction Processing Council (TPC). The council is one of several organizations formed to develop and control standard benchmarks. The TPC benchmarks are actually a set of specifications for how the standard benchmarks should be run. Usually the hardware vendors create, run, and publish the results of a TPC benchmark, usually in hopes of using their results to win sales. The hardware vendor chooses the DBMS to be used for the benchmark.

The TPC offers specifications for several types of benchmark tests:

- TPC Benchmark A—TPC-A is the earliest test specification, introduced in 1989, modeling a banking transaction. A series of simple SQL statements (a few UPDATE statements and an INSERT statement) are executed with a think time to simulate users.

- TPC Benchmark B—TPC-B is the same as TPC-A, except that it has no simulated user interaction. Transactions are submitted one after another with no think time.

- TPC Benchmark C—TPC-C is a more complex OLTP benchmark specification, which makes it a little more realistic than the TPC-B benchmark. It models an order-entry environment and offers a variety of multirow database operations instead of the same transaction executed repeatedly.

- TPC Benchmark D (decision support)—TPC-D is a benchmark specification that is geared towards complex queries.

Usually, hardware vendors will publish a transactions-per-second figure, relating it to a cost of hardware, software, and maintenance. However, there is much more valuable information available in the full disclosure that is required. You can get the full disclosure from the hardware vendor that conducted the test or from the Transaction Processing Council for a fee.

You can use the TPC benchmarks for several purposes:

- To evaluate hardware platforms. For example, if your production system is heavily transaction-oriented, you may examine the TPC-B performance numbers on several hardware platforms in order to choose the best one for your needs.

- To evaluate hardware upgrades. If the same hardware vendor has published performance numbers on both the older and newer hardware configurations, you can compare the benchmark results between the two to estimate the amount of increased capacity you can experience in your production system.

- To evaluate database products. The major database vendors publish TPC results on the major hardware platforms. Although the benchmark results should not be the only deciding factor in a database purchasing decision, it can be one factor.

Since TPC benchmarks are very generalized, *they should not replace your own custom tests.* Many potential database customers require the database vendor to participate in a custom benchmark test that more completely represents the customer's application and database requirements.

2.12   EVALUATING PERFORMANCE—PERFORMANCE TOOLS AND MONITORS

Even if you are monitoring performance of a database product, you cannot examine its behavior without taking into account the behavior of the operating system and hardware. For example, if database INSERTS are slow, you might examine the disk I/O. Perhaps the disk is handling its capacity, and the data should be spread across multiple disks. As another example, if your system is short on memory, you may see disk access increase as well because pages in memory are written to disk during swapping or paging operations to make room for other pages.

Unfortunately, every UNIX machine varies in what kind of monitoring tools it offers. You should examine your operating system documentation for more information. However, for your information, here is a summary of some tools that are offered on various operating systems and hardware platforms. We will discuss how these tools can be used in various situations throughout the book.

vmstat

The **vmstat** tool reports information on process, memory, CPU, and some disk activity. Besides the command line options, **vmstat** has two parameters which you will almost always include, interval and count. The following example will show intervals of every two seconds, ten times:

```
vmstat 2 10
```

The first line in the report shows the activity since the system was last booted. The remaining lines show activity for the interval.

Here is sample output of **vmstat**.

```
%vmstat 2 3
procs   memory        page         disk      faults   cpu
r b w avm  fre  reatpipofrdesrd0d1d2d3insy   csussyid
0 0 0 0    2060 0 7 0 0 2 160 0 0 0 0 7 75   173 1 96
0 0 0 0    2052 0 284 0 240 9 150 0 0 72269  61218 71
0 0 0 0    2052 1 250 0 120 5 8 0 0 0 72256  607 8 85
```

iostat

The **iostat** utility provides more information on disk activity. The **iostat** utility works similarly to **vmstat** in that each line represents activity for a time interval. Here is some sample output of iostat:

```
% iostat 2 5
tty dk0 dk1 cpu
   tin  tout bps tps  msps bps  tps  msps us   ni   sy   id
   0    0    3   0    0.0  1    0    0.0  2    0    1    96
   0    25   0   0    0.0  0    0    0.0  10   0    1    89
   0    25   66  10   0.0  0    0    0.0  23   0    9    68
```

ps

The **ps** command is a powerful tool to get a snapshot of memory and CPU usage at a particular point in time. The **ps** command can differ in format and options, but generally, the following information can be listed for each process in the UNIX system:

- The percentage of CPU currently being used
- The percentage of memory currently being used
- The amount of memory currently being used
- The status of the process (running, idle, etc.)
- The priority of the process ("nice" value)

sar

The **sar** utility lists information about CPU usage, disk usage, and many other interesting facts about a system. Some systems may have the **sar** utility, but not the **vmstat** and **iostat** utility.

A simple sar output that shows CPU usage every five seconds is shown below.

```
%sar 5 5

10:06:22 %usr %sys %wio %idle
10:06:27 34    1    0    65
10:06:32 34    2    0    64
10:06:37 34    1    0    65
10:06:42 17    1    0    82
10:06:47 1     1    0    98
```

Graphical Tools

Some hardware vendors offer graphical representations of performance. For example, Sun Microsystems offers **perfmeter**, a tool that gives you a graphical representation of CPU activity, paging activity, and disk activity. Hewlett-Packard offers HP/UX Glance, a very useful graphical performance monitor. Sequent Computer systems has **monitor**, which displays a real-time monitor of activity on the system.

It is important when using these kind of tools to remember that they may be using some CPU themselves to run. Some can run the graphical front-end on a different system than they are reporting on. Also, you must make sure you understand exactly what each graph or report is depicting.

Informix Utilities

Informix offers two utilities helpful to performance tuning: **tbstat** and **tbcheck**. The **tbstat** utility actually reads shared memory for a snapshot of information about the OnLine system. Some of the information that can be obtained in version 5.0 is listed below.

```
-a print all info
-b print buffers
-c print configuration file
-d print dbspaces and chunks
-h print buffer hash chain info
-k print locks
-l print logging
-m print message log
-p print profile counters
-s print latches
-t print tblspaces
```

```
-u print users
-z zero profile counts
-B print all buffers
-C print btree cleaner requests
-D print dbspaces and detailed chunk stats
-R print LRU queues
-x print transactions
-X print entire list of sharers and waiters for buffers
```

You can reset many of the shared memory counters in these options by running **tbstat -z**. This is useful for tuning purposes when you want to measure activity for a certain interval of time. These counters are also reset when the OnLine system is brought down and back up.

Version 6.0 changes the name of the utility to **onstat**. It also offers a myriad of other parameters that show you what is happening in the multithreaded subsystem. Some of these options are interesting but not really useful for tuning.

```
-g xxx (xxx is one of the following options)
all print all MT information
ath print all threads
wai print waiting threads
act print active threads
rea print ready threads
sle print all sleeping threads
spi print spin locks with long spins
sch print VP scheduler statistics
lmx print all locked mutexes
wmx print all mutexes with waiters
con print conditions with waiters
stk <tid> dump the stack of a specified thread
glo print MT global information
mem <pool name|session id> print pool statistics.
seg print memory segment statistics.
rbm print block map for resident segment
nbm print block map for non-resident segments
afr <pool name|session id> print allocated pool fragments.
ffr <pool name|session id> print free pool fragments.
ufr <pool name|session id> print pool usage breakdown
iov print disk IO statistics by vp
iof print disk IO statistics by chunk/file
```

```
ioq print disk IO statistics by queue
iob print big buffer usage by IO VP class
ppf [<partition number> | 0], print partition profiles
tpf [<tid> | 0], print thread profiles
ntu print net user thread profile information
ntt print net user thread access times
ntm print net message information
ntd print net dispatch information
nss <session id> print net shared memory status
nsc <client id> print net shared memory status
nsd print net shared memory data
sts print max and current stack sizes
dic print dictionary cache information
qst print queue statistics
wst print thread wait statistics
prc print procedure cache information
dsc print data distribution cache information
ses <session id> print session information
sql <session id> print sql information
dri print data replication information
```

When tuning a system, you may want to store **tbstat** (**onstat**) reports and reports from system utilities in a file. This is a simple (yet important) matter of redirecting the output to a file.

```
onstat -p >> results.out
```

You can also run the **tbstat** (**onstat**) option every *n* seconds and redirect the output to a file, for example:

```
onstat -r 10 -p >> results.out
```

In version 6.0 Informix added an SQL interface, called the *System Monitoring Interface* (SMI), which can be used to retrieve most of the information that can be gathered with **tbstat** (**onstat**). The SQL interface allows you to retrieve the information easily within a program or the DB-Access utility, and display it or store it in a history table.

The SMI "tables" are stored in a database called **sysmaster**, which is created automatically at initialization time or when the OnLine system is converted to version 6.0. The SMI tables don't actually contain data; instead, they store a pseudo-table id that is recognized internally by OnLine and used to access the actual data in shared memory.

Although there are quite a few SMI tables, the tables and views that are supported by Informix are listed below, along with the **onstat** option, which gives similar information:

```
sysdatabases- Databases in the OnLine system
systabnames- Tables within all databases
syslogs - Logical log information (onstat -l)
sysdbspaces - Dbspace information (onstat -d)
syschunks - Chunk information (onstat -d)
syslocks - Lock information (onstat -k)
sysvpprof - Virtual processor information (onstat -g glo)
syssessions - Session information (onstat -g ses)
syssesprof - Session level profile information (onstat -g ses)
sysextents - Extent information
syschkio - I/O statistics by chunk (onstat -D)
sysprofile - System profile information (onstat -p)
sysptprof - Tblspace profile information (onstat -t)
```

You can get a listing of columns for these tables by selecting the **sysmaster** database in the DB-Access utility and choosing the **Table:Info** option.

While **tbstat** (or **onstat** in 6.0) and SMI principally read statistics found in shared memory, the **tbcheck** (**oncheck** in 6.0) utility reads information found in disk structures. Although **tbcheck** is used mainly for problem diagnosis, there are a few options that are useful for viewing the layout of data on disk. The **tbcheck** (oncheck) options are listed below:

```
r - reserved pages (-cr)
e - extents report (-ce)
c - catalog report (-cc)
k - keys in index (-ci)
K - keys and rowids in index (-cI)
l - leaf node keys only (-ci)
L - leaf node keys and rowids (-cI)
d - TBLSpace data rows (-cd)
D - TBLSpace data rows including bitmaps, remainder pages
and blobs (-cD) t - TBLSpace report
T - TBLSpace disk utilization report
p - dump page for the given [table and rowid | TBLSpace and
page number] P - dump page for the given chunk number and
page number
```

```
B - BLOBSpace utilization for given table(s) [data-
base:[owner.]]table
```

Another way of monitoring activity (not just performance) is to read the OnLine message log. The message log is just a file that stores diagnostic messages about the activity of the OnLine system. **tbstat -m** will give the pathname and list the last ten lines of the message log.

Some of the messages that can be displayed in the message log are shown in the example below.

```
15:44:20 INFORMIX-OnLine Initialized -- Shared Memory Ini-
tialized
15:44:20 Physical Recovery Started
15:44:20 Physical Recovery Complete: 0 Pages Restored
15:44:20 Logical Recovery Started
15:44:20 Logical Recovery allocating 10 worker threads
('OFF_RECVRY_THREADS').
15:44:25 Logical Recovery Complete
   0 Committed, 0 Rolled Back, 0 Open, 0 Bad Locks


15:44:26 Tbconfig parameter BUFFERS modified from 200 to
1000
15:44:26 Tbconfig parameter LRU_MAX_DIRTY modified from 60
to 95
15:44:26 Tbconfig parameter LRU_MIN_DIRTY modified from 50
to 85
15:44:26 Quiescent Mode
15:44:26 Checkpoint Completed: duration was 0 seconds
15:44:38 On-Line Mode
15:45:17 Logical Log 7 Complete
15:49:36 Checkpoint Completed: duration was 8 seconds
```

2.13 CONFIGURATION PARAMETERS

The principal method for tuning an OnLine system is through a set of configuration parameters. They are stored in a file under the directory **$INFORMIXDIR/etc**. The file can have an arbitrary name; OnLine finds it through an environment variable you set called TBCONFIG (ONCONFIG for 6.0). There is one configuration file for every OnLine system or instance running on the machine.

For the most part, the configuration parameters are read once before the OnLine system comes up. Therefore, you can change the configuration parameters anytime while the OnLine system is up, but the new parameters will not take affect until the next time the OnLine system is brought down and back up.

To change configuration parameters, you can either edit the file or use the **tbmonitor** (**onmonitor** in 6.0) utility, which is a more user-friendly menu interface to the configuration file.

Chapter 3

Database Design

$\mathbf{Y}$ou can tune the hardware, the operating system, and the OnLine system; but if the database is not designed properly, you will not receive optimal performance. This chapter gives an overview of the important performance issues in designing an OnLine database. Some of the database design and implementation issues discussed in this chapter include:

- Transaction logging
- Indexing
- Normalization
- VARCHAR columns
- BLOB columns
- Stored procedures and triggers
- Release 6.0 database design issues

3.1   TRANSACTION LOGGING

Databases in an OnLine system can have one of three logging options: no logging, unbuffered logging, or buffered logging. The option you choose can affect performance of the database and the OnLine system. A discussion of these options follow.

No Logging

A database with no logging means that any Data Manipulation Language (DML) statements, such as INSERT, UPDATE, or DELETE statements, for that database are not recorded in the logical log and cannot be rolled back. The implications of an unlogged database should be understood very clearly should you decide to create one.

1. An application connecting to an unlogged database cannot take advantage of the concept of a *transaction*. A transaction is a set of SQL statements that are effectively treated as one operation. If one SQL statement in the transaction fails, all SQL statements in the transaction will be rolled back as if they never happened. Without logging, the BEGIN WORK and COMMIT WORK statements in an application will cause an SQL error to occur.

2. If the machine crashes, or the OnLine system fails for any reason, what you thought to be completed may not actually have been completed. Without logging, the database will be restored to the time of the last checkpoint (which could be five to ten minutes before the crash), effectively wiping out all completed operations since that time.

3. If, for some reason, you must restore from an archive, no roll forward can occur since the OnLine system has not recorded transactions. You will only be able to recover back to the point of the last archive.

Having said this, it is important to note that a database with no logging performs faster in database update operations than a database that is logged. If your database holds noncritical information or if data can be reloaded from an external source if necessary, then by all means, don't log the database. For example, a phone company holding switch data that is used for reporting trend information may not care if a portion of the data is lost.

No logging is the default mode when a database is created. To change a database with logging to no logging for version 5.0, run the following command:

```
tbtape -N database_name
```

In version 6.0, run:

```
ontape -N database_name
```

Buffered Logging

For more critical data, you will probably want to turn logging on. The most efficient form of logging is *buffered logging*. With this option, all of the database update activity is recorded in the form of transaction entries in the *logical log*. The logical log is an area on disk created and controlled by OnLine specifically for recovery purposes. To cut down on the number of disk writes required to the logical log, the log entries are placed in a memory buffer, called the *logical log buffer*. The default size of this buffer is 32k, but it is tunable with the LOGBUFF configuration parameter. When the buffer is full, it will be flushed to the logical log file on disk. The logical log buffer is also flushed during a checkpoint.

Because OnLine is writing to disk in 32k chunks, buffered logging is the most efficient of logging forms. However, there is a drawback. You can lose transactions that you
thought were committed if they are in the logical log buffer and the OnLine system or the
machine goes down for any reason.

You can specify that a database have buffered logging when you create it using the
following syntax:

```
CREATE DATABASE database_name
    WITH BUFFERED LOG
```

You can also change a database from unbuffered logging to buffered logging once
the database has been created with the **tbtape** command (in version 6.0, substitute **tbtape**
with **ontape**).

```
tbtape -B database_name
```

If you want to start logging on a database that has no logging, you must initiate an
archive at the same time that the logging is changed.

```
tbtape -s -B database_name
```

Unbuffered Logging

The safest yet most inefficient form of logging is unbuffered logging (see Figure
3.1). Databases with unbuffered logging cause the logical log buffer to be flushed any time
a transaction is committed. This could be after one statement, or several in a longer transaction that uses BEGIN WORK and COMMIT WORK. Control is not returned to the user
when a transaction is committed until the buffer is written to disk. Unbuffered logging
means that you will never lose a committed transaction if the system goes down. It also
means that the logical log will be one of the most I/O-intensive areas on disk and that
overall performance, especially for smaller transactions, will be affected.

Note that since all databases in an OnLine system share the same logical log buffer,
databases with buffered logging will be affected by any database that has unbuffered logging in that the buffer will be flushed every time a transaction commits on the database
with unbuffered logging.

You can specify that a database has unbuffered logging when you create it, using
the following syntax:

```
CREATE DATABASE database_name
    WITH UNBUFFERED LOG
```

You can also change a database from buffered to unbuffered logging once the database has been created with the **tbtape** command (**ontape** in version 6.0).

```
tbtape -U database_name
```

If changing from no logging to unbuffered logging, an archive must be performed at the same time that logging is changed.

```
tbtape -s -U database_name
```

Figure 3.1-   Buffered vs. unbuffered logging

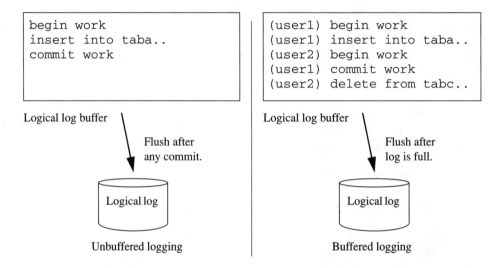

3.2   ANSI DATABASES

An ANSI database complies to ANSI specifications. You specify that a database is ANSI in the CREATE DATABASE statement.

Administrators choose to use an ANSI-compliant database because it conforms to certain standard behaviors. Applications accessing any ANSI database can expect it to act in certain ways. One of the behaviors of an ANSI database is that it must have unbuffered logging. Also, applications are required to be in transaction at all times. BEGIN WORK is implicitly invoked starting when the database is accessed and immediately after a COMMIT WORK is executed in the application. This and other behaviors directly affect locking, and hence, the performance of the database server. For example, read locks (locks held on data that is accessed in a SELECT statement) will be held until the end of the transaction in an ANSI database.

Unless standards are important to your organization and you are willing to compromise performance for those standards, do not create an ANSI database.

3.3   INDEXING

Indexes are used to improve the time it takes to access data in a table. It can affect not only query performance, but performance on UPDATE, INSERT, and DELETE statements as well. To understand the implications that indexes have on performance, it is important to know how they work.

Informix database servers use b+ trees to create the indexes (hereafter referred to *b-trees*). The special feature of this kind of b-tree is that it is always balanced. In other words, it always takes a set number of index reads to retrieve the data, no matter where the key lies in the b-tree.

A b-tree has a number of levels. The *root*, or *level-0* node, will be the starting point of any user trying to locate a row. The levels under that are *level-1*, *level-2*, and so on. The nodes on the lowest level, or *leaf nodes*, have pointers to the actual data pages that hold the row. Each node is the size of a page.

To find a row, start at the level-0 node and find the key value that is less than or equal to the value for which you are searching. Follow the corresponding pointer to the level-1 node. For each node, repeat the process until you find the leaf node. From the leaf node you can retrieve the actual address of the data page.

How many levels the b-tree has depends on the number of rows the table has, the size of the index, and how full the b-tree nodes are. Very small tables may only have two b-tree levels. Very large tables may have four or five levels. Every level in the b-tree requires an extra read to get to the data. A b-tree with three levels (as shown in Figure 3.2) requires three reads to get to the leaf level, and another read is needed to actually get the data. Some of these reads may be from memory because of OnLine's disk caching. However, a large index usually requires one or two disk reads for each random row read.

With a SELECT statement, you will usually be reading only one index for each table. However, with any UPDATE, DELETE, or INSERT statement, all indexes may be read.

- An INSERT statement adds a new row and consequently, a new entry in the b-tree for every index. If a table has three indexes with three levels each, an INSERT statement will effectively cause nine index reads!

- An UPDATE of a b-tree key effectively consists of a DELETE of the old key and an INSERT of the new key. An UPDATE statement only updates the columns listed in the UPDATE statement. If a column listed in the UPDATE statement has an index, the b-tree for that index will be read. An index b-tree will not be read on columns that are not included in the column list in the UPDATE statement. That's why it's very important to list only the columns you are changing in an UPDATE statement.

- A DELETE statement must read all b-trees to delete the key for each row that will be deleted.

Figure 3.2-   An index B-tree

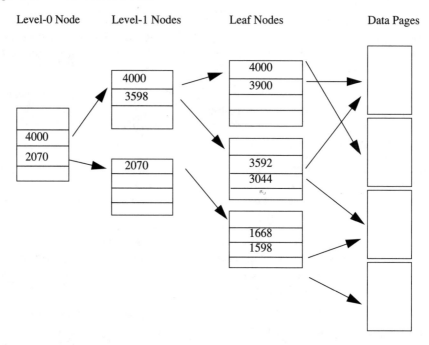

You can see from this discussion that, although indexes may improve query performance, they will affect other SQL operations negatively. You must decide where optimal performance is more important, in query operations or update operations. Most administrators try to strike a balance between the two by only creating the minimal number of indexes on tables that might satisfy the important queries.

3.4   IMPROVING PERFORMANCE WITH INDEXES

Putting indexes on important columns will keep OnLine from having to read a table sequentially.

Generally, you will add at least one index for each table, on the primary key. In fact, the PRIMARY KEY designation will automatically put an index on the table. For example:

```
CREATE TABLE account(
    account_nbr      SERIAL PRIMARY KEY,
    last_name        CHAR(20),
    first_name       CHAR(20),
    account_balance MONEY(12,2))
```

This statement automatically creates an index on the account number column.

Another common column to index is any *foreign key*. A foreign key is a column that is used to join one table to another. This type of relationship is also known as *referential integrity*. For example, the **account** table may have a relationship to the **transaction** table, which may have the following schema:

```
CREATE TABLE transaction(
    transaction_id  SERIAL PRIMARY KEY,
    account_nbr     INTEGER REFERENCES
                        account(account_nbr),
    transaction_amt MONEY(12,2);
```

The REFERENCES keyword specifies that this column is a foreign key. The **transaction** table uses **account_nbr** as a foreign key that relates the transaction table to the primary key, **account_nbr**, in the **account** table. An index will automatically be put on a foreign key column, which will be useful for any query operations that join the two tables.

For more information on the ramifications of using referential integrity, consult your Informix documentation.

Once you decide what columns to index, there are some guidelines you can follow to create and monitor indexes.

Monitor Index-Page Fullness

An optimal index for queries would be one that has full b-tree pages. With full pages, one disk read will bring into memory the most key values possible. Also, with full pages, you have no more b-tree levels than absolutely necessary. However, excessive b-tree splits or key deletes may cause index pages to become near-empty. With a sparsely packed index, more disk reads may be required to bring the needed key values into memory.

You can monitor the index-page fullness by running:

```
tbcheck -pT database:table
```
Or, for version 6.0, run:

```
oncheck -pT database:table
```

At the bottom of the report, information about each index is listed. For each b-tree level, the number of pages for that level and the average number of free bytes per page are listed. A sample listing for an index is shown below.

```
Index Usage Report for index iaccount on db:x.account
                  Average  Average
   Level Total   No.Keys  Free Bytes
   ----- -------- -------- ----------
     1     1        4       1973
```

| 2 | 4 | 116 | 506 |
3	466	128	217
Total	471	128	223

In the example above, the leaf pages have an average of 217 free bytes, which means they are approximately 90% full (assuming a 2k byte page size). This is a very good average, especially if the table is being updated frequently. If the average free bytes drops below approximately 30–40% of the page size, you might see some improvement by dropping the index with the DROP INDEX statement and re-creating it with CREATE INDEX.

When the index is re-created, OnLine will try to fill each index page completely (6.0 OnLine behaves differently, as explained later in this chapter), so you may see a dramatic decrease in the average number of free bytes in the leaf nodes after the index is rebuilt. If the index rebuild caused fewer b-tree levels, you have decreased the number of reads every user must perform for the index by at least one!

Once you rebuild the index, and all pages are full, any new INSERTS will cause a full index page to *split*. This means that one index page will be split into two pages, with each page taking half of the keys of the original page (see Figure 3.3). After the index is rebuilt, you may see early INSERT performance degradation (because of the high number of splits occurring) and a quick decline in the fullness of a page. There's not much you can do about this, except to be aware that it will happen and (if feasible) occasionally rebuild the index. In version 6.0, you can control how much to fill index pages during an index build, as explained later in this chapter.

Figure 3.3-   Index pages before and after a split

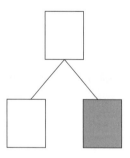

Before the split, the index
page is full.

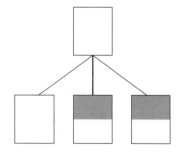

After the split, each index page is
only half-full.

Keep Key Sizes to a Minimum

By including only the necessary columns in a composite index (an index containing more than one column) and making sure the column sizes are not excessive, you can cut down on the key size and therefore put more keys on one page. With more keys on one page, hopefully fewer pages will have to be read from disk.

Avoid Highly Duplicate Indexes

A highly duplicate index is one that has a large number of duplicate keys, and can severely affect performance for UPDATE and DELETE statements. For example, suppose you have an index on a **customer_type** column, and there are only five possible **customer_type** codes. If the table has one million rows, there could potentially be 200,000 rows with the same type code. The b-tree would store the key value, followed by a list of pointers to each of the physical rows. The problem occurs when you have to DELETE or UPDATE the key value. OnLine must search through the duplicates until it finds the correct key to delete!

To identify highly duplicate indexes, run the following statements on every database:

```
update statistics;
select tabname,idxname,nrows/nunique duplicates
   from systables,sysindexes
   where systables.tabid = sysindexes.tabid
   and systables.tabid >99
```

This SELECT statement will give you an average number of duplicates per key value for each index. To pinpoint a specific highly duplicate value, you will have to actually examine the contents of the row. Or, with version 6.0, you can create a distribution on the column with UPDATE STATISTICS and examine the distribution of data values for that column.

To avoid the performance bottleneck of a highly duplicate index, create a composite key with the highly duplicate column and a more unique column. The example below shows the avoidance of a highly duplicate key by adding the **customer_num** column:

```
CREATE INDEX key_1 on customer
   (customer_type,customer_num)
```

Perform Occasional Checks on the Fitness of the Index

You may want to check that the index is not corrupted, especially if users are complaining about query performance. If an index is corrupted, OnLine will not use it. You can check indexes for each table by running the following **tbcheck** command (**oncheck** for version 6.0) or dropping and re-creating the index:

```
tbcheck -cI database:table
```

3.5   NORMALIZATION

Database design can fundamentally affect the performance of any application using that database. It is important to thoughtfully design a database so that you can make effective use of SQL in an application.

One of the common methods of grouping data in such a way that it is better suited to the relational model is often referred to as *normalization*. Although it is beyond the scope of this book to explain normalization, we will discuss when you might want to denormalize a database schema. Denormalization is when a table might deliberately break the rules of normalization to achieve better performance.

A fully normalized database allows for *flexibility*, most specifically in querying for data. Denormalizing data may make it more difficult to retrieve data cleanly using SQL.

However, a normalized database also tends to be one with a larger number of tables and rows. Because of that, some database designers tend to denormalize to increase performance. Some of the more common denormalization strategies are listed below.

Store Derived Values

A derived value is a value that is created by a calculation involving values of other columns. A common example of a derived value is an account balance. Instead of calculating the account balance by reading all transaction rows for an account, you can keep a running total of the balance.

An example of a normalized version of an account and transaction table is:

```
create table account(
   account_nbr    integer,
   first_name     char(30),
   last_name      char(30));

create table transaction(
   transaction_id  serial,
   account_nbr     integer,
```

```
amount          money(12,2),
...
);
```

To obtain an account balance for an account with the normalized schema, you would execute an SQL statement such as:

```
select sum(amount) from transaction
  where account_nbr = 22
{Multiple rows must be selected for result}
```

An example of a denormalized version of an **account** and **transaction** table that stores a derived value is:

```
create table account(
    account_nbr    integer,
    first_name     char(30),
    last_name      char(30),
    balance        money(12,2));
```

```
create table transaction(
    transaction_id  serial,
    account_nbr     integer,
    amount          money(12,2),
    ...
    );
```

To obtain an account balance for an account with the denormalized schema, you would execute an SQL statement such as:

```
select balance from account
  where account_nbr = 22;
{One row is selected for result}
```

One disadvantage of storing derived values is that the balance may get out of sync with the transactions. In our example you can prevent this from happening by using an INSERT, UPDATE, and DELETE trigger on the transaction table to automatically update the **account** table. This strategy takes the responsibility away from the programmer to correctly code the update of the **balance** column.

Another disadvantage of storing derived values is that you will have to perform another UPDATE of the derived value table for every change in the dependent table. In our example, for every INSERT of the **transaction** table, one UPDATE of the **balance** column for the **account** table is required.

Store Repeating Groups in One Row

A repeating group is a list of columns within a table that are essentially other instances of the same column. An interesting example of repeating groups is student grades for four grading periods in a year. In a normalized table, each grade would be stored in its own row, so four rows must be selected to get a student's grades for a year. You can denormalize the table by putting all grades in one row, thereby causing a selection of only one row to get the year's grades.

An example of a normalized **grades** table is:

```
CREATE TABLE grades(
   student_id     INTEGER,
   year           DATETIME YEAR TO YEAR,
   quarter        SMALLINT,
   grade          CHAR(1),
   );
```

To retrieve grades for a student using the normalized table, you would run an SQL statement such as:

```
SELECT quarter, grade FROM grades
   WHERE student_id = 33
   ORDER BY quarter;
{Multiple rows are retrieved and must be ordered by
quarter}
```

An example of a denormalized **grades** table, with a repeating grades column is:

```
CREATE TABLE grades(
   student_id     INTEGER,
   year           DATETIME YEAR TO YEAR,
   quarter1_grade  CHAR(1),
   quarter2_grade  CHAR(1),
   quarter3_grade  CHAR(1),
   quarter4_grade  CHAR(1));
```

To retrieve grades for a student using the normalized table, you would run an SQL statement such as:

```
select quarter1_grade,quarter2_grade,
   quarter3_grade,quarter4_grade
   from grades
   where student_id = 33
{Only one row is retrieved}
```

Although this query might actually run faster with the denormalized table, you have to consider other queries that might be executed. For example, finding the average grade for all students is very simple with the normalized table, but much more difficult with the denormalized model.

Split Tables

When separate parts of a table are used by different applications, the table can safely be split into two tables. The advantage of this technique is that the row size for the individual tables are smaller, and more rows can fit on a page.

For example, suppose a table that stores information about hotels in a hotel chain has the following rows:

```
CREATE TABLE hotel(
    hotel_nbr          INTEGER,
    hotel_name         CHAR(30),
    nbr_rooms          SMALLINT,
    hotel_city         CHAR(20),
    hotel_state        CHAR(2),
    mgr_lname          CHAR(20),
    mgr_fname          CHAR(20),
    hotel_phone        CHAR(12),
    hotel_address      CHAR(80),
    hotel_directions   VARCHAR(60,200));
```

If there is some information that is rarely used in a table, you can split that information into another table. For example, if customers rarely ask for the directions and the address of the hotel, you can split that information into another table.

```
CREATE TABLE hotel(
    hotel_nbr          INTEGER,
    hotel_name         CHAR(30),
    nbr_rooms          SMALLINT,
    hotel_city         CHAR(20),
    hotel_state        CHAR(2),
    mgr_lname          CHAR(20),
    mgr_fname          CHAR(20),
    hotel_phone        CHAR(12),
    );
CREATE TABLE directions(
    hotel_nbr          INTEGER,
    hotel_address      CHAR(80),
    hotel_directions   VARCHAR(60,200));
```

After the split, the row size for the **hotel** table is decreased by potentially 284 bytes. This means that more rows for the **hotel** table can fit on one page, increasing the chances that a needed row will be in memory rather than on disk.

However, if the majority of applications access both tables, this methodology will probably decrease performance, because both tables will have to be accessed.

3.6   HOW TO APPROACH DENORMALIZATION

As you can see from these examples, there is a sizable risk involved in denormalizing a database design. It is very important when considering denormalization that you determine how the applications will use the data and whether performance will improve enough to warrant the inconvenience of a denormalized table.

Follow these guidelines when considering denormalizing a database:

1.   Determine response time requirements. For example, if users are expecting response times of less than five seconds for queries, you may be able to meet that requirement without denormalizing. Remember that imperceptible performance enhancements won't be recognized and applauded by the user population!

2.   Perform a benchmark to determine the performance behavior of a normalized database.

3.   Denormalize only if benchmarks do not provide the required response time. Even then, you must also determine how denormalization will affect the response time of the query you are studying, but also *any other operation that will affect the denormalized table*.

As table denormalization can affect how applications are developed, it is important to make denormalization decisions well in advance of the application development stage.

3.7   EFFECTIVE USE OF VARCHAR

Using the VARCHAR character type in some cases may be a great performance enhancement. Some column types have wildly variable sizes. A good example of this is any kind of comments column. You usually make a comments column very large so that it can fit the largest comment. However, some rows will have short comments, and many will have none at all. OnLine always allocates the maximum amount of space for each CHAR column, whether it is used or not, so when comments are not used, quite a bit of disk space is wasted.

An example of creating a table with a VARCHAR column is:

```
CREATE TABLE customer_call(
   customer_id INTEGER,
   date_called DATETIME YEAR TO MINUTE,
   reason_code CHAR(2),
   comments    VARCHAR(10,256));
```

You specify two values when creating a VARCHAR column: the minimum size and the maximum size. The minimum size specifies the minimum number of bytes that will be reserved for the column. The maximum size specifies the largest size the column can reach. If the column is empty, only the minimum number of bytes will be allocated. In the example above, only ten bytes will be reserved for a row with no comments.

Using VARCHAR appropriately will decrease the average row size, allowing more rows to be stored in each data page. The more rows there are per page, the fewer overall disk reads will be required to retrieve the rows.

3.8 EFFECTIVE USE OF BLOB COLUMNS

A *BLOB* (Binary Large OBject) column is used to store unstructured information, such as documents, video, document images, and pictures. There are two types of BLOB columns, BYTE and TEXT. The TEXT column type should be used to store text documents. The BYTE column type should be used to store all other documents with nontext data.

You have two choices as to how to store BLOB columns, in the table or in a separate dbspace called a *blobspace*. The choice you make could have a significant impact on over-all OnLine system performance.

BLOB columns stored in the table are actually stored in different pages in the extents where the data pages are held. When a BLOB stored in a table is inserted or updated, it is logged in the logical and physical log, just as regular data is. The BLOB pages are also brought in through the buffer cache. As you can imagine, if the BLOB itself is very large, it strains the logical and physical log resources, and causes caching problems in the buffer pool as well.

To create a BLOB stored with the rest of the table, use the IN TABLE keywords in the CREATE TABLE statement; for example:

```
CREATE TABLE document(
   document_id SERIAL,
   document    BYTE IN TABLE
   );
```

Alternatively, BLOB columns can be stored in a separate blobspace. Not only does the storage location change, but also the treatment of the BLOB pages. When this kind of BLOB is inserted or updated, it is not stored in the logical log or physical log, nor is it brought through the buffer pool (other methods are used to ensure recovery in case of a failure).

To create a BLOB column stored in a separate blobspace, include the blobspace name in the CREATE TABLE statement; for example:

```
CREATE TABLE document(
    document_id SERIAL,
    document    BYTE IN blobsp1
    );
```

Because BLOBs stored in a separate blobspace avoid the standard logging and buffer mechanism, they are an excellent vehicle for large BLOBs. BLOBs of only a couple of pages can safely be stored with the rest of the table.

Another advantage of storing large BLOB columns in a separate blobspace is that the administrator can specify the BLOB page size for each blobspace. By using a larger BLOB page size, large BLOBs can be stored contiguously on disk, rather than in multiple pages in different locations within the extent.

3.9   STORED PROCEDURES AND TRIGGERS

Stored procedures are pieces of application code that actually reside in the database. The advantage of stored procedures is that they can cut down on the number of messages passed back and forth between the application process and the database server. Also, the SQL inside a stored procedure is pre-optimized, so this step is not required during execution.

It turns out that a stored procedure has its own overhead, including being read from the database and being converted into an executable format. Because of this overhead, stored procedures do not always enhance performance. Generally, they will improve performance in one or more of these cases:

- The stored procedure contains more than two or three SQL statements. Multiple SQL statements in a stored procedure decrease the amount of message traffic and spread the overhead of a stored procedure over multiple statements.

- The network is slow. If the network is slow, using stored procedures to reduce the amount of message traffic can improve performance.

Triggers are SQL statements that can be executed whenever an INSERT, UPDATE, or DELETE is executed on a certain table. Triggers can effectively improve performance in the same way as stored procedures, especially when they cut down on the number of SQL statements in an application.

3.10   6.0 DATABASE DESIGN CHANGES

There are a few changes in the 6.0 version of INFORMIX-OnLine Dynamic Server that may alter performance for your database design.

Increased Index Size

The size of the index will probably increase because of the change in index key locking. Each key item uses one extra byte for *key value locking*. Key value locking is a new type of locking where a key value being deleted is not deleted until after the transaction is committed. When you convert an OnLine system to 6.0 from 5.0, you may see extra pages allocated for each index because of the extra byte allocated per key.

Unfortunately, there is nothing you can do about this increase in size; however, it may be offset by the change in the way index pages are filled when they are created.

FILLFACTOR

When an index is built using version 5.0, the b-tree pages are filled to capacity. Since the keys are sorted first, this means that most of the pages are filled to 100% capacity, meaning the b-tree is extremely compact. This is extremely efficient for any query operations using the recently built index, because more keys are packed in one page. However, as soon as an INSERT occurs, there is no room to place the key on the page, and the b-tree page must be split into two pages, each approximately half full. Given enough random INSERTs, the index b-tree can go from being extremely compact to being half-full and inefficient. Also, the original INSERT statements can perform poorly because of the extra work required to perform the split.

In version 6.0, you can specify the amount of space in each index page that will be filled during an index build with a configuration parameter and an addition to the CREATE INDEX syntax. This change will allow you to create an index with room to add key values later, which can minimize the number of index b-tree splits that occur once rows start to be added to the table.

The configuration parameter is called FILLFACTOR. This is the default fill factor of all indexes that are created unless otherwise specified in the CREATE INDEX statement. The example below shows FILLFACTOR set at 90%.

```
FILLFACTOR   90
```

To override the default fill factor for a particular index, specify the FILLFACTOR in the CREATE INDEX statement. The example below will create index pages filled to 100% capacity.

```
CREATE INDEX ix_1 ON customer(customer_num)

FILLFACTOR 100;
```

For static tables, or tables that only have deletions, you should use a FILLFACTOR of 100. Most other tables can use the default FILLFACTOR. There may be some cases where you may want to decrease the FILLFACTOR to 60–70% if the table will be receiving a large number of new rows.

You can monitor the fullness of an index with the **oncheck** command.

```
oncheck -pT database:table
```

The fill factor primarily affects the leaf nodes. The following table was created with 100% fill factor:

```
Index Usage Report for index icustomer on db1.customer
```

Level	Total	Average No. Keys	Average Free Bytes
-----	--------	--------	----------
1	1	3	1986
2	3	139	214
3	417	143	5
-----	--------	--------	----------
Total	421	143	11

You can use this output to adjust the fill factor. Run and save the output of the **oncheck** command after the index is built. After a period of activity, run **oncheck** again and check the average free bytes and total number of index pages. The average free bytes should have increased.

Remember that once an index is created, the fill factor is no longer in effect. Eventually, as INSERTS occur, index pages will fill and begin to split. The fill factor is only effective for a limited period of time.

3.11 DATABASE CONFIGURATION CHECKLIST

Table 3.1- Database configuration checklist

What to Check	How to Check	How to Alter
Database logging	tbmonitor—the **Status:Database** option.	**tbtape**, or by dropping and re-creating the database with a different logging option
Index page fullness	tbcheck -pT *database:table*	DROP INDEX and CREATE INDEX
Minimum key size	dbschema -d *database*	ALTER TABLE to change the column size. DROP INDEX and CREATE INDEX to change a composite key
Highly duplicate keys	Examine the **nunique** column in **systables** or the contents of each row.	DROP INDEX and CREATE INDEX using a more unique key (perhaps through a composite key)
Fitness of an index	tbcheck -cI *database:table*	tbcheck or DROP INDEX and CREATE INDEX
Effective use of VARCHAR	Examine contents of large character columns	ALTER TABLE
BLOB column (large BLOBs stored in separate blobspaces)	dbschema -d *database*	ALTER TABLE
FILLFACTOR (version 6.0)	N/A	Alter FILLFACTOR configuration parameter or DROP INDEX and CREATE INDEX with new fill factor

Chapter 4

Disk Performance

Disk reads and writes are two of the highest-cost operations in any computer system. They are also an inevitable part of a database management system. Your goals to improve disk performance should be twofold: First, try to avoid or curtail these operations as much as possible; second, if the I/O is necessary, try to spread the work evenly across disks and over time.

Some of the topics that will be discussed in this chapter include:

• Disk and memory reads

• Monitoring and tuning the read cache rate

• Monitoring and tuning disk writes

• Disk arrangement considerations

• Disk tuning with the 6.0 release

4.1   DISK AND MEMORY READS

OnLine reads database information in units of pages, either 2 Kbytes or 4 Kbytes, depending upon the system. Reads can occur not only for database SELECTs, but also for any UPDATE and DELETE—OnLine must read the page with the data before it can be deleted or updated.

If the needed page is in the shared memory buffer cache, it will be read from memory. If it is not in memory, the page is read from disk and put in the shared memory buffer cache. Since the buffer cache is shared, many users can access the same page. The more often data is read from memory and not disk, the higher the read "cache" rate. Systems with a high cache rate are obviously more desirable.

4.2   MONITORING READ CACHE RATE

You can monitor the read cache rate by running **tbstat -p** (**onstat -p** for 6.0). The first **%cached** field shows the read cache rate since the OnLine system was brought up, or since the statistics were cleared with **tbstat -z** (**onstat -z**). In the example excerpt from the **-p** report below, the read cache rate is 99.48%, a very good percentage.

```
Profile
dskreads  pagereads bufreads  %cached dskwrits  pagwrits  bufwrits  %cached
2383      2389        453962    99.48   14776     20943     77792     81.01
```

The cache rate is calculated for you in this report, but you can calculate the read cache rate yourself by using the following formula:

$$100 * (bufreads - dskreads) / bufreads$$

The read cache rate can vary dramatically, depending upon the applications and the type and size of the data being operated on. If users are accessing the same data constantly, the read cache rate can potentially be very high. If data access is very random and the database is large, the read cache rate might be lower, say, in the 70–80 percentile.

However, there are some steps you can take to make sure the read cache rate is optimal for your OnLine system.

4.3   TUNING READ CACHE

You tune the cache rate primarily by decreasing or increasing the number of shared memory buffers allocated to the buffer cache, with the BUFFERS configuration parameter. By increasing the buffer cache, you allow more pages to stay in memory. Why not add the highest amount of buffers allowed? Because each buffer takes up space in memory either 2 Kbytes or 4 Kbytes. This means that each buffer takes up at least 2 Kbytes or 4 Kbytes of memory. Although a database entirely in memory would get great performance, this probably won't be possible on average size systems if your database is larger than 30 or 40 megabytes.

The best you can do is to increase the number of buffers until your read cache rate stops increasing dramatically, or you reach the memory constraints of your system. We will be discussing memory issues in a later chapter, but for now, let's concentrate on the buffer cache. To tune the cache rate, follow these steps:

1.   Reset the statistics with **tbstat -z** (**onstat -z** for 6.0).

2.   Run several hours or days of typical live production. Tuning cache rate during live production is preferable since it is hard to simulate production data access in a benchmark test.

3.   Record the cache rate in percentage from **tbstat -p**.

4.   Increase the buffers configuration parameter and bring the OnLine system down and back up.

5.   Repeat steps 2 through 4 until there is no increase in the read cache rate.

4.4   DISK AND MEMORY WRITES

There are a set of processes, called *page cleaners*, that are responsible for writing pages from the buffer cache to disk. In version 6.0 the page cleaners are threads, and they pass the buffer write requests to the AIO vp. Page cleaners do this work either during a check-point or between checkpoints if the buffer cache gets too full of "dirty" pages (pages that have been changed since they were read from disk).

The buffer pages are organized into a set of linked lists, called Least Recently Used (LRU) queues (see Figure 4.1). Each queue is subdivided into a clean queue and a dirty queue. Pages in the clean queue are available for being overwritten by other users. Pages in the dirty queue must be written to disk before they can be reused. When a database server process needs to read a page from disk, it finds a buffer from the least-recently-used end of the clean LRU queue and replaces its contents with the contents of the page read from disk. The buffer is then put on the most-recently-used end of the LRU queue. This mechanism is useful to keep the pages that are used quite often from being overwritten by new pages read from disk.

Figure 4.1-   LRU queue

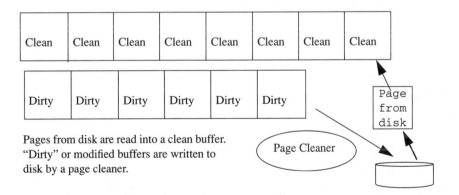

Pages from disk are read into a clean buffer. "Dirty" or modified buffers are written to disk by a page cleaner.

When a page is written to in memory, it is marked as dirty, meaning its contents have been changed and it must eventually be written to disk. During a checkpoint, which is nothing more than a synchronization between what is in memory and what is on disk, all dirty pages will be read from memory to their respective location on disk.

Between checkpoints, OnLine needs to guard against all of the buffers becoming dirty—once a buffer is dirty, it cannot be written to again until the contents are flushed to disk. Occasionally, the LRU queues are examined for dirty pages. If a certain percentage of pages within the LRU queue are dirty, the page cleaner will write the dirty pages to disk.

From this discussion you can see that there are two times that pages can be written to disk: **during a checkpoint**, and **between checkpoints**. The ideal situation is that we would never write to disk. If we could always perform database operations in memory, we would have 100% cache rate and the best performance. Two things stop us from doing so: the database is probably larger than the buffer cache, and recovery would take a long time if the system crashed.

You could tune the OnLine system to have it write most, if not all, dirty pages to disk only during the checkpoints. This might increase the cache rate somewhat, as you are giving database server processes time to potentially write to a page in memory more than once. If a page is modified in memory more than once, the overall cache rate will improve and, potentially, the overall OnLine system performance. The problem with this is in the way a checkpoint occurs. When a checkpoint begins, all database server processes are prevented from entering "critical sections" of code, which means they must wait to do some things, such as writing to pages. If the checkpoint duration is long, this could have some serious implications on performance.

So when might you want to write to disk between checkpoints? There are some valid situations. If the buffer cache cannot hold all the pages that will be altered between checkpoints, some writing must take place. Also, since a checkpoint stops all writes from occurring until the checkpoint is completed, you might see some delay in processing if there are a large number of dirty pages that must be written.

The top diagram in Figure 4.2 shows the performance of a system that relies on most disk writes to occur during a checkpoint. The disk devices will show a spike in activity during a checkpoint and erratic activity between checkpoints. The bottom diagram shows the possible performance of a system that relies on a mixture of disk writes during a checkpoint and between checkpoints. Although there is still some spike of activity during checkpoints, the overall disk activity is more stable and spread more evenly throughout processing.

Figure 4.2-   Disk Activity (a) without writes between checkpoints and (b) with writes between checkpoints

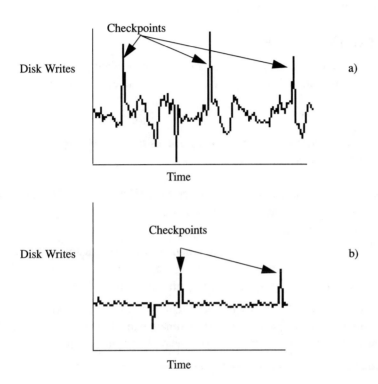

By spreading disk activity out between checkpoints, you may see a more even response time for users. You may even see better throughput because the shorter checkpoints will not delay transaction activity. However, the write cache rate may decrease somewhat, since OnLine may be writing pages more often to disk. Consider a page that is updated five times between two checkpoints. Using the formula shown previously, you can calculate the write cache rate for the one page as:

```
100 * (5 - 1) / 5 = 80%
```

If the page is written to disk once between checkpoints, however, the cache rate becomes:

```
100 * (5 - 2) / 5 = 60%
```

If the reality in your system is that pages are written many times during a checkpoint, it would probably be better to perform most disk writes at checkpoint time. If the writes are more random across a larger number of pages, it is best to spread the disk writes evenly between and during checkpoints.

4.5   TUNING DISK WRITES

You have a great deal of control, through a series of configuration parameters, over how and when pages get written to disk. These configuration parameters are explained below.

Checkpoint Interval

The *checkpoint interval* is the number of seconds between checkpoints. There are several ways to tune the checkpoint interval.

1.   The CKPTINTVL configuration parameter sets the default interval. Set this to the maximum number of seconds between checkpoints.
2.   A checkpoint will also occur when the physical log is 75% full.

You can determine the frequency of checkpoints by running **tbstat -m** (**onstat -m**). The **-m** option lists the last few lines of the message log. To view more lines of the message log, you can edit the message log itself (the path name is listed in the report heading).

Every time a checkpoint occurs, a line is written to the message log with the time the checkpoint occurred. You can calculate the approximate interval between checkpoints by subtracting the time of one checkpoint from the time of the previous checkpoint.

Here is an excerpt of sample output from the message log.

```
Message Log File: /home/informix/5.00/online.log
15:49:36 Checkpoint Completed
15:54:48 Checkpoint Completed
```

In this example (although you should check more than one interval), the checkpoint frequency is about five minutes.

Instead of setting the checkpoint interval by the CKPTINTVL, consider driving the checkpoint interval by the physical log size. For example, you can set CKPTINTVL to a large number, say, 15 minutes, and set the physical log file to cause a checkpoint to occur every 10 minutes with average activity. This strategy causes checkpoints to occur when there has been sufficient database activity, *not* at a certain time interval.

You can check the current log size by looking at the PHYSFILE configuration parameter. You can increase the physical log size by running the **tbparams** utility.

```
tbparams -p -s log-size
```

A large checkpoint interval may make the process of recovery longer. If the OnLine system goes down for any reason, all pages in the physical log must be reapplied. With a large physical log, this may take anywhere from several seconds to 20 minutes, depending upon the physical log size. Start with the checkpoint interval as high as possible without making the recovery process too long, usually somewhere between 5 and 15 minutes. There is no good way to estimate how long recovery will take given a checkpoint interval. The estimation varies between hardware platforms and the number of transactions that must be rolled forward.

LRU Queues

The number of LRU queues can be configured. Since each user can access an LRU queue to read a page or move it within the queue, it is important to configure enough LRU queues to decrease contention for the queues by users and page cleaners. Generally, the number of LRU queues you have will not have a great effect on performance, unless you have configured too few.

Setting LRUS in Version 5.0

You can set the number of LRU queues the buffers are assigned to by the LRUS configuration parameter. Only one database server process at a time can alter an LRU queue. If you set the LRUS parameter too small, the database server processes will compete for the LRU queue. If you set the LRUS parameter too high, it will require more internal administrative work to keep track of a large number of queues. A rule of thumb is to configure LRUS to 3 + the number of processors in your system. With more processors, more database server processes can be accessing the LRU queues at once.

Setting LRUS in Version 6.0

The LRU queues are only accessed by threads running within the CPU virtual processors. This means that the amount of contention on LRU queues depends on how many CPU vps are configured (how to configure CPU vps will be discussed in a later chapter). Generally, you want to configure as many LRU queues as CPU vps, starting with at least four.

Page Cleaners

The page cleaner processes in version 5.0 are responsible for writing pages to disk. In version 6.0, the page cleaner threads are responsible for gathering modified pages and submitting the write request to the AIO sub-system.

During a checkpoint, each page cleaner is assigned one or more chunks. The pages are first sorted by chunk and the location within the chunk. Then they are written. Between checkpoints, the page cleaners are assigned to LRU queues, and the page cleaners write out the dirty pages in random order from the LRU queue (see Figure 4.3).

Figure 4.3-   Page cleaners and checkpoints

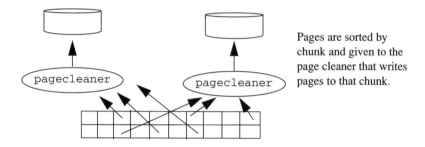

Pages are sorted by chunk and given to the page cleaner that writes pages to that chunk.

Setting CLEANERS for Version 5.0

How you set the number of page cleaners (CLEANERS configuration parameter) depends upon two things: the number of disks and the number of LRU queues allocated. During a checkpoint, it is best to have approximately the same number of page cleaners as disks. The number of page cleaners determines the degree of parallelism during checkpoint writes. If CLEANERS is set to five, the number of disks that can be written to simultaneously is five.

An important thing to remember is that the OnLine system does not know if you have two chunks on the same disk. It will assign chunks to page cleaners in a round-robin fashion. The first chunk that was created goes to page cleaner 1, the second chunk to page cleaner 2, and so on. This means that you should pay special care to how chunks are created at initialization time. For example, if the OnLine system has three disks with two chunks each, you should create chunk 1 on disk 1 first, chunk 2 on disk 2 second, chunk 3 on disk 3 next, chunk 4 on disk 1 next, and so on. With this scheme, each page cleaner would most likely be cleaning a separate disk, rather than having two or more page cleaners writing to the same disk at once while other disks remain idle.

The optimal number of page cleaners for writes between checkpoints is somewhat different, however. You should have approximately the number of page cleaners as you have LRU queues (see the following section for information about setting the number of LRU queues). This is because a page cleaner is assigned at any one time to clean an LRU queue. Having more page cleaners than LRU queues is probably overkill.

Given these two different guidelines for setting page cleaners, which one should you pick? If the majority of disk writes occur between checkpoints, configure the number of page cleaners using the second method (CLEANERS = LRU queues). If the majority of disk writes occur at checkpoint time, configure the number of page cleaners using the first method (CLEANERS = disks). You may then increase or decrease the number of page cleaners slightly to see if it improves performance.

CLEANERS for Version 6.0

The number of page cleaners needed for a system in version 6.0 will probably decrease because there is less contention for the queues between CPU vps. Because of this, you can set CLEANERS to the number of disks that will be updated during a checkpoint. However, if LRUS is set higher than the number of disks, set CLEANERS to LRUS. Having more CLEANERS than LRU queues should not hurt performance.

4.6   LRU CONFIGURATION PARAMETERS

There are other configuration parameters used to determine when and how many writes occur between checkpoints. LRU_MAX_DIRTY is the maximum number of pages that must become dirty before the page cleaners start to clean. The LRU_MIN_DIRTY parameter is the percentage of the queue that the page cleaner will leave dirty.

As an example, if LRU_MAX_DIRTY is set to 80 and LRU_MIN_DIRTY to 60, the page cleaners would wake up when 80% of the queue consists of dirty pages. The page cleaners would write dirty pages to disk until only 60% of the pages are full, as shown in Figure 4.4.

Figure 4.4-   LRU_MAX_DIRTY and LRU_MIN_DIRTY example

Dirty	Dirty	Dirty	Dirty	Dirty	Dirty	Dirty	Clean	Clean

If LRU_MAX_DIRTY is 80% and LRU_MIN_DIRTY is 60%, then a page cleaner would write two dirty pages to disk from this queue.

One of the things that the LRU parameters affect is the *checkpoint duration*, the time it takes to complete a checkpoint. It is difficult to determine the checkpoint duration in version 5.0. However, you can run **tbstat -r 2**, which will print the status line every two seconds, and wait for the CKPT designation to appear in parentheses after the mode. When the CKPT designation disappears (or when the checkpoint message is written to the log), the checkpoint is complete.

In version 6.0, you can determine accurately how long a checkpoint lasted with the **onstat -m** option or by editing the message log. The checkpoint duration is listed next to each checkpoint log entry, for example:

```
16:44:50 Checkpoint Completed: duration was 7 seconds
16:49:55 Checkpoint Completed: duration was 3 seconds
16:54:44 Checkpoint Completed: duration was 0 seconds
```

If checkpoint durations are long, you may try to decrease them by decreasing the LRU_MAX_DIRTY and LRU_MIN_DIRTY parameters so that more pages are written between checkpoints.

To minimize the checkpoint duration, set LRU_MIN_DIRTY and LRU_MAX_DIRTY to small values, such as 5 and 10. This setting would keep the page cleaners working most of the time between checkpoints. Hopefully, by the time the checkpoint occurs, most of the pages are clean.

If you prefer to have most of the disk writes occur during the checkpoint, set LRU_MIN_DIRTY and LRU_MAX_DIRTY to larger values, such as 90 and 98.

Monitoring LRU Queues in Version 5.0

You can monitor the LRU queues in version 5.0 with the **tbstat -R** command. A sample of the relevant part of the output is shown below.

```
4 buffer LRU queues
LRU 0:    8 (40%) modified of 20 total
LRU 1:    4 (26.7%) modified of 15 total
LRU 2:    5 (26.3%) modified of 19 total
LRU 3:    7 (36.8%) modified of 19 total
24 dirty, 73 queued, 75 total, 32 hash buckets, 2048 buffer size
start clean at 60%, stop at 50%
```

From this output you can see that there are four LRU queues (LRUS set to 4). Between checkpoints, page cleaning will start when the queue has 60% dirty buffers (LRU_MAX_DIRTY = 60) and will stop at 50% (LRU_MIN_DIRTY = 50). During a checkpoint, all pages will be cleaned.

The number in parentheses is the percentage of the queue that is dirty. You can see this number rise as pages are written to in memory by database server processes and fall as pages are written to disk by page cleaner processes.

Another interesting command is **tbstat -F**. The output of this command can be used to determine how many writes occurred during checkpoints and how many writes occurred between checkpoints. An example of the interesting part of **tbstat -F** is shown below.

```
Fg Writes  LRU Writes  Idle Writes  Chunk Writes
   31          212         18891         341
```

The **Fg Writes** column specifies the number of writes that occurred because the database server process failed to find a clean buffer to read a page into, and consequently wrote a dirty buffer to disk itself. This type of write is very inefficient, as the user will be delayed while the database server process performs the write.

LRU Writes are writes that generally occur when the database server process relocates a page on the LRU queue and notices that the percentage of dirty pages exceeds LRU_MAX_DIRTY. Also, after 16 fg writes have been performed, the master daemon will cause the page cleaners to wake up and clean the queues. These writes are classified as LRU writes as well.

Idle Writes are any writes that occur during normal page cleaner activity between checkpoints.

Chunk Writes are the writes performed by page cleaners during checkpoints.

In the sample **tbstat -F** output, most of the disk writes (18891) occurred between checkpoints.

If you want to perform most writes between checkpoints, you should try to decrease the chunk writes and the fg writes and increase the idle writes and LRU writes. You can cause this to occur by decreasing the LRU_MAX_DIRTY and LRU_MIN_DIRTY parameters.

Monitoring LRU Queues in Version 6.0

You can monitor the LRU queues in version 6.0 with the **onstat -R** command. A sample of the relevant part of the output is shown below.

```
8 buffer LRU queue pairs
# f/m    length  % of pair total
0 f         29    58.0%       50
1 m         21    42.0%
2 f         38    76.0%       50
3 m         12    24.0%
4 f         17    34.7%       49
5 m         32    65.3%
6 f         34    68.0%       50
```

```
7  m        16    32.0%
8  f        23    43.4%      53
9  m        30    56.6%
10 f         0     0.0%      50
11 m        50   100.0%
12 f        27    57.4%      47
13 m        20    42.6%
14 F        44    88.0%      50
15 m         6    12.0%
187 dirty, 399 queued, 400 total, 512 hash buckets, 2048 buffer size
start clean at 70% (of pair total) dirty, or 5 buffs dirty, stop at
60%
```

Each line in this output represents either the free buffers or the modified (dirty) buffers in a queue. The **length** is the number of buffers, and the **% of pair** is the percentage of the LRU pair that is either clean or dirty.

From this output you can see that there are eight LRU queues (LRUS set to 8). Between checkpoints, page cleaning will start when the queue has 70% dirty buffers (LRU_MAX_DIRTY = 70) and will stop at 60% (LRU_MIN_DIRTY = 60). During a checkpoint, all pages will be cleaned. In the first queue pair, 58% of the buffers (29) are free, and 42% of the buffers (21) are dirty. You can see the percentage of modified or dirty buffers rise as pages are written to in memory by the session threads and fall as pages are written to disk by the AIO subsystem.

The **onstat -F** command can be used to determine how many writes occurred during checkpoints and how many writes occurred between checkpoints. An example of the interesting part of **tbstat -F** is shown below:

```
Fg Writes    LRU Writes   Chunk Writes
0            38226        3030
```

The **Fg Writes** column specifies the number of writes that occurred because a session failed to find a clean buffer to read a page into, and consequently submitted a request to write a dirty buffer to disk itself. This type of write is very inefficient, as the user will be delayed while the AIO subsystem performs the write.

LRU Writes are writes that generally occur when the percentage of dirty pages on a queue exceeds LRU_MAX_DIRTY between checkpoints. Also, after 16 fg writes have been performed, the page cleaners wake up and clean the queues. These writes are classified as LRU writes as well.

Chunk Writes are the writes performed by page cleaners during checkpoints.

In the sample **onstat -F** output, most of the disk writes (38226) occurred between checkpoints.

If you want to perform most writes between checkpoints, you should try to decrease the Chunk Writes and the Fg Writes and increase the LRU Writes. You can cause this to occur by decreasing the LRU_MAX_DIRTY and LRU_MIN_DIRTY parameters.

Buffer Pool Size

The buffer pool size is the number of pages from disk that can be put in shared memory. The BUFFERS configuration parameter specifies the number of pages in the buffer pool. This parameter will affect your write cache rate, the percentage of time data is written to memory rather than to disk. It will also affect the LRU configuration. As you increase the size of the buffer pool, more pages will be assigned to each LRU queue. For example, if BUFFERS is set to 1000 and LRUS is set to 10, each LRU queue will handle 100 pages. If LRU_MAX_DIRTY is set to 80%, page cleaning will start when 20 pages have been modified. However, if you increase the buffer pool size to 2,000, each LRU queue will handle 200 pages, and page cleaning will start when 40 pages are dirty.

You monitor the write cache rate in the same way as the read cache rate, with **tbstat -p** (**onstat -p** in version 6.0). In the example report below, the write cache rate is 81.01%. As does the read cache rate, the write cache rate varies depending on the applications and the type and size of the data being operated on.

```
Profile
dskreads   pagereads bufreads   %cached dskwrits   pagwrits   bufwrits %cached
2383       2389      453962     99.48   14776      20943      77792    81.01
```

4.7   DISK ARRANGEMENT CONSIDERATIONS

The previous discussion has centered on how to alter the operation of OnLine once the system is initialized and the disk layout was set. Additionally, you should consider the placement of tables and other OnLine structures on disk. If disk arrangement is poor, some disks may be overly busy, while others may remain idle. Your OnLine performance will suffer as a result. Ideally, you want to spread the workload evenly across disks.

4.8   HARDWARE ISSUES

There are two issues in disk throughput. One is how fast data can be read from and written to disk. The other is how much data can be written to disk during a certain period of time. The I/O speed depends on the seek time, rotational speed, and transfer rate of the disk itself. Obviously, a faster disk will perform better when a process is reading and writing a large amount of data. When there are many users accessing data, more disks are generally better. However, disk controllers can be a bottleneck if they control access to multiple disks. Discuss with your hardware vendor the best mix of disks to disk controllers.

Some disks support transparent disk striping. The effect of striping can be a chunk that actually spans disks in relatively small pieces. OnLine will support this kind of disk as long as the disk striping is completely transparent to a UNIX read() and write() call. They can be very effective in dividing a large table across disks. You may see a performance gain with disk striping during sequential read operations or when many users are using the same chunk. However, as a note of caution, don't run out and buy a disk like this if you are planning to migrate to later versions of OnLine that support disk fragmentation. Disk striping may actually hurt performance in later versions of OnLine if you use the disk fragmentation feature.

4.9   OTHER DISK USAGE

Before planning disk layout for OnLine data, consider the other disk activity in your system. One important segment of disk for all systems is the swap area, the pages in memory that get copied out to disk. In most cases, the swap area should be on the faster disks and, if possible, spread across multiple disks. For very busy systems, the disks containing swap space will be very busy as well.

If there is any other disk activity on your system, you should isolate the disks that contain the busy filesystems, if possible.

4.10   RAW DEVICE OR FILESYSTEM?

Informix recommends that you use raw devices for your chunk. The recommendation is for two reasons. First, the OnLine data is not subject to the levels of indirection a highly fragmented filesystem may encounter. With high levels of indirection, the data for a table may reside on different places on a disk, and your performance will suffer on sequential reads. Second, the filesystem contains its own buffering mechanism, which can be good for many applications, but not necessarily for database applications. When OnLine gets a return value from a write call, it expects the data to be on disk. With buffering on filesystems, the page may still be in a memory buffer somewhere, not on disk. Having said that, there are two points to mention. The first point is that some operating systems support a synchronous write call (with the O_SYNC flag), and OnLine will most likely use that if it is present in your system. The second point is that you may actually get better performance with the filesystem (assuming a minimum of filesystem indirection) because of the very efficient read-ahead capabilities that some systems have.

The safest alternative, and one that will provide generally good performance in all cases, is to use raw devices.

4.11   PLACEMENT OF ONLINE OBJECTS ON DISK

Here are some factors you need to minimize when choosing the layout of your dbspaces:

1.   The amount of time it takes for the disk head to reach the data, often called *seek time*

2.   Access to the disk by multiple requestors, or *disk contention*

3.   Which disks the controller accesses, or disk *controller contention*

As a general rule, you want to decrease the seek time for data that is accessed more often. How do you do this? When you choose the center tracks on a disk, the disk head will not have to travel very far in either direction to get to these tracks (see Figure 4.5). When a disk is partitioned, you specify a set of cylinder numbers for each device. The cylinder numbers in the middle of the range usually denote the center tracks. A device using these cylinder numbers should be reserved for high-priority disk access.

Figure 4.5-   The center tracks on disk

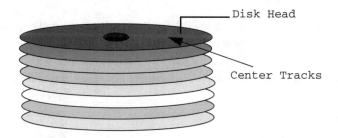

The second factor, disk contention, means that multiple processes are trying to access the same disk at one time. Only one request can be completed at a time per disk, so the other requestors must wait. To cut down on disk contention, you can spread the data that OnLine must access across several disks.

The third factor is the disk controller contention. In many systems, one disk controller can service the requests for multiple disks. In addition to cutting down on disk contention, you need to minimize disk controller contention. Find out which disks are serviced by each controller, and keep that in mind when spreading data across disks.

Physical and Logical Logs

For applications where there is a great deal of data being updated, the physical and logical log placement is important. For decision support applications, the physical and logical log can take lower priority in disk placement. Why are the physical and logical log so important? For every write, an entry goes in the logical log buffer. The logical log buffer gets flushed to disk:

1.   When it is full.

2.   For databases created with unbuffered logging, when a transaction is committed. It
      is very important that these writes occur quickly because users may be delayed until
      the writes occur.

      Also, a before image of a page is put in the physical log buffer the first time it is
updated between checkpoints. The physical log buffer is flushed to disk:

1.   When it is full.

2.   Whenever page cleaners flush any changed pages to disk. It is imperative that the
      before image of a page be put on disk before its corresponding changed page is writ-
      ten.

The Root Dbspace

It is a good practice not to place any databases or tables in the root dbspace. The root
dbspace contains some essential control information about the OnLine system. In version
5.0, the root dbspace will also be used for temporary tables (created with SELECT INTO
TEMP). In version 6.0 of OnLine, temporary tables can be redirected to another dbspace.

The Tables

The goal in placement of database tables is to spread the I/O workload across disks
and controllers. You specify the dbspace in which the table will be placed using the CRE-
ATE TABLE statement. Once you define the location with CREATE TABLE, you cannot
change the location except by dropping the table and re-creating it. That is why it is
important to spend some time analyzing the optimal location of tables on disk.

Before deciding where tables should be placed, perform an analysis of the applications that access the tables. How often are each of the tables accessed during peak periods? What tables are accessed together? From this information, you can now begin to
diagram a possible strategy for table placement.

You can perform your own striping by storing a table across several disks. Large
tables will be spread across disks anyway because the data won't fit on one disk. To stripe
a table, create a dbspace and add chunks on each disk. The example in Figure 4.6 shows a
dbspace (**dbspace1**) with three chunks, with each chunk on a separate disk. The table **t1** is
created in **dbspace1**. When rows are added to table **t1**, they will be added to the extent that
will be created in the first free chunk, **chunk1**. When the first extent is filled, OnLine will

create a new extent on the first free chunk; if the first chunk does not have enough free space to hold the extent, it will be created on the second chunk. You do not have any direct control over which chunk the rows are created in.

Figure 4.6- Striping a table across disks

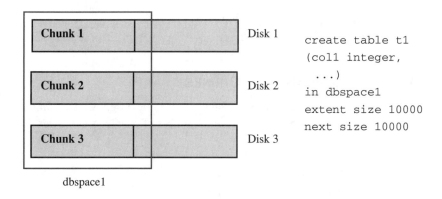

```
create table t1
(col1 integer,
   ...)
in dbspace1
extent size 10000
next size 10000
```

From this discussion it follows that if **t1** starts out small, the rows will only be located on one disk. You will not receive any striping benefits until the table grows. However, you can "trick" the OnLine system into placing the second and third extents in disk 2 and 3 by creating dummy tables with large extent sizes in **dbspace1**. Say, for example, that each chunk is 25 megabytes. Table **t1** is created with the first extent of 10 megabytes. If you create a dummy table with an extent of 10 megabytes, this reserves 10 megabytes of space that cannot be used for table **t1** (you do not have to add any rows to the dummy table). When table **t1** needs another extent, it will be created on the next free chunk, **chunk2**, because there are not 10 megabytes of free space on **chunk1**! You can later drop the dummy table as t1 grows across three disks.

If you have many small to medium-size tables that are heavily used, you may not want to stripe tables. For example, if 50 users are all executing a transaction that updates four tables on two disks, each table is being accessed approximately the same amount. By putting two tables on one disk and two tables on another disk, you are effectively spreading the work evenly across disks without striping. As shown in Figure 4.7, this disk layout would require only two dbspaces.

Figure 4.7-   Table layout without striping

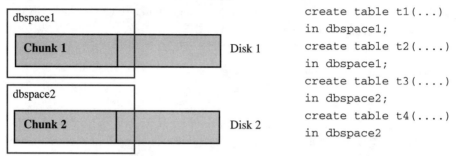

```
create table t1(...)
in dbspace1;
create table t2(....)
in dbspace1;
create table t3(....)
in dbspace2;
create table t4(....)
in dbspace2
```

4.12   LIMIT ON THE NUMBER OF CHUNKS

The limitation on the maximum number of chunks in version 5.0 may constrain the way you configure disks. In version 5.0, the maximum number of chunks is the lower of these two values:

1.   The number of chunk pathnames that can fit onto a page. One page keeps both the chunk name and the location (pathname) of the chunk of disk for all chunks in the OnLine system. One way to allow more chunks in the OnLine system is to keep the chunk pathnames to a minimum. If you are using raw devices, you should use a symbolic link to the device name.Symbolic links can help shorten the device name as well as being a good idea in case the disk goes down and needs to be replaced (you can relink the symbolic name to another disk device). For example:

```
ln -s /dev/rsd01e /I/chk1
```

2.   The number of available file descriptors that can be used by a process. This is an operating system limit. On most versions of UNIX, you can increase the open files per process by adjusting a UNIX kernel parameter.

The first limitation may keep the number of chunk pathnames down to approximately 30 to 40 chunks. This might not seem like a limitation, but this means that with ten disks used for OnLine, only three or four chunks can be created on each disk. This severely limits the amount of disk striping you can implement at the OnLine system level for large databases.

In version 6.0, the limit on the maximum number of chunks is 2,048.

4.13   EASE OF ADMINISTRATION

With more dbspaces and chunks in an OnLine system, the administrator has to pay closer attention to the free space in each dbspace. Remember that an ALTER TABLE statement often must create a complete copy of the table being altered in the same dbspace as the one in which the table resides. With one table per dbspace, you don't have a pool of free space in which to perform an ALTER TABLE. Also, with more dbspaces, you must monitor each to make sure there is enough free space allocated to handle the growth in a table. If one table grows more than you expected, you may have to rearrange dbspaces to obtain more space for the larger table.

Rearranging usage of dbspaces is difficult. To reassign disk space from one dbspace to another, you must drop a chunk (only allowed in version 6.0) or dbspace and re-add that space to another dbspace. However, the chunks that are being dropped must be completely empty, meaning you must first drop the tables that have extents in that chunk before dropping the chunk. A better way to manage growth of tables is to leave some empty disk space unassigned to dbspaces. If more space is needed, you can simply add a new chunk using the previously unassigned disk space.

4.14 DISK PLACEMENT PRIORITIES

As a review, here are the priorities in disk placement of the various components of an OnLine system. For decision support systems (emphasis placed on queries) or databases without logging:

1. Most used tables
2. Least used tables
3. Logical and physical logs

For transaction-oriented systems:

1. Logical and physical logs
2. Most used tables
3. Least used tables

With one disk, there are not many choices in the placement of the OnLine structures. Figure 4.8 shows three dbspaces, one for the root dbspace, one for the logical and physical logs, and one for the data.

Figure 4.8-   Sample disk layout with one disk

root dbspace	logs dbspace	tables dbspace

For two disks and an OnLine system that has OLTP activity, you can put the root dbspace and the logical and physical logs on one disk, and the data on another (see Figure 4.9). Another strategy is to put some tables on disk 1 and some tables on disk 2.

Figure 4.9-   Sample disk layout with two disks

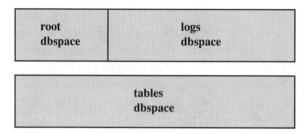

For three or more disks, you have more choices (see Figure 4.10). For high OLTP systems with a large database, it would benefit you to place the logical logs on their own disk. The reasoning behind this philosophy is that the writes to the logical log are sequential. The disk head would be placed in the correct position at all times to write to the logical log if there is nothing else placed on that disk. If the logical logs don't take up the full disk, consider putting infrequently used tables in a dbspace on the same disk.

Figure 4.10- Sample disk layout with three or more disks

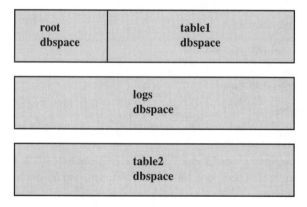

4.15 MONITORING DISK LAYOUT

Once you get data loaded into your proposed disk layout, you can check the results of your work by running **tbstat -D** (onstat -D in 6.0). With the output from this command you can see the I/O that occurred on each chunk since the last time the OnLine system was brought down, or since the last **tbstat -z** (onstat -z) cleared the statistics.

A sample output from this command is shown below.

```
Dbspaces
address    number  flags  fchunk  nchunks  flags  owner     name
818480       1       1       1       1        N    informix  rootdbs
818480       2       1       2       1        N    informix  dbs2


2 active, 8 total


Chunks
address    chk/dbs    offset   page Rd    page Wr    pathname
817e94      1   1       0       31082      199065    /dev/chunk6
817f2c      2   2       0        2520        3807    /dev/chunk7
2 active, 8 total
```

The **page Rd** and **page Wr** columns show the amount of disk reads and writes for all the tables in each chunk. You cannot determine the amount of I/O for each table, unless the dbspace only holds one table. Some administrators put highly used tables in their own dbspaces just to get this information.

In the example above, chunk6, which belongs to the root dbspace, is receiving most of the disk reads and writes. Your next step after seeing this output is to determine what OnLine objects are in **chunk6**. The **tbcheck -pe** command (**oncheck -pe**) can be used to see the exact contents of the chunk. To even out the I/O between these two chunks, you could move some objects in the root dbspace to dbs2.

You should also monitor disk I/O at the UNIX level with the **sar** or **iostat** utility, to get an idea of the disk utilization levels.

4.16   SPECIAL CONSIDERATIONS FOR THE 6.0 RELEASE

In version 6.0, the I/O is controlled by a set of I/O vps. The LIO vp handles logical-log I/O. The PIO vp handles physical-log I/O. The AIO vps handle all other I/O, both reads and writes, on behalf of the sessions and the page cleaners. The page cleaner processes in version 5.0 become threads running on the CPU vps in version 6.0.

On some operating systems, the actual disk I/O is handled not by the AIO vps, but by the UNIX kernel. This type of I/O is known as *kernel AIO*, and can add a significant performance boost to I/O processing. However, it is only used for OnLine I/O on certain systems. Check the machine notes file in the **$INFORMIXDIR/release** directory to determine whether kernel AIO is being used or not. Even if the product supports it, kernel AIO will be used only on chunks that were created using raw devices. Chunks created on file system files (or cooked chunks) will continue to use the AIO vps.

The AIO vps monitor their queue for requests and service each request, performing the I/O by reading dirty pages from the buffer pool and writing them to disk.

The 6.0 release offers a set of different/new parameters that should be tuned. They are:

- Number of AIO vps
- Read-aheads

Number of AIO VPs

If your OnLine system is using kernel AIO for all I/O, configuring the number of AIO vps is easy. The AIO vps will only be used for I/O to files such as the $ONCONFIG file or the message log. You need only configure one or two AIO vps—one for a smaller system, two for a larger system.

If you have chunks residing on file system files (not raw devices) or your OnLine system does not use kernel AIO, configuring the number of AIO vps becomes very important. You do not want AIO vps to have a long backlog of requests for I/O. You can monitor the backlog of AIO requests by running **onstat -g ioq**. This command shows the current length of the I/O queue (**len**) for each of the AIO vps and the largest the AIO queue has ever been (**maxlen**). Since each AIO vp has its own queue, the report will show one line for every AIO vp. A sample output of **onstat -g ioq** is listed below, showing two AIO queues.

class/hvp-id	len	maxlen	totalops	dskread	dskwrite	dskcopy
adt	0	0	0	0	0	0
msc	0	0	1	3	0	0	0
aio	**0**	**0**	**150**	**26725**	**18589**	**8136**	**0**
aio	1	0	150	1254	940	314	0
pio	0	0	0	0	0	0	0
lio	0	0	0	0	0	0	0

A clever indication that the OnLine system is using kernel AIO is the appearance of a kio queue in this output. If you see the kio queue and you are using raw devices, set the number of AIO vps to 0.

To monitor the AIO queues, bring up the OnLine system, and then run **onstat -z** to clear out statistics (the queue length becomes abnormally high when the OnLine system first comes up), and then monitor the **len** and **maxlen** columns over a period of time. You may notice that the queues for the AIO vps farther down the list have a max queue length of 0, or close to 0. This is because of the way the requests are put on a queue. The threads look through each vp's queue, looking for a place to put a set of I/O requests. If the queue is empty, the set of requests is put there. If not, the next queue is examined. If the later queues are empty most of the time, this means that a thread was able to find an empty queue in one of the first vps. However, if the current queue lengths are often greater than 0, you can try adding an AIO vp.

You can configure the number of AIO vps by the NUMAIOVPS configuration parameter or by dynamically adding AIO vps while the OnLine system is up using **onmonitor**.

Read-Aheads

The optimal behavior of the OnLine system is for a session reading data to never have to wait for a disk read. The best way to cut down on disk reads is to somehow second-guess the next page that the user will need and read it from disk into the buffer pool before the page is requested by a user. This mechanism is called *read ahead*. OnLine will perform a read-ahead under several circumstances:

1. The optimizer senses that a SELECT will perform a sequential scan. An example of a SELECT that will probably perform a sequential read:

   ```
   SELECT * from tab1
   ```

2. The optimizer senses that a SELECT will read the index sequentially, and that all of the needed columns are part of the index. Another term for this case is a key-only search. An example of a SELECT that will probably perform a key-only search (assuming **col1** has an index) is:

   ```
   SELECT col1 from table1 where col1 > 200
   ```

3. The optimizer senses that a SELECT will read the index sequentially, but must retrieve the data page as well. An example of this kind of SELECT (assuming col1 has an index):

   ```
   SELECT * from table 1 where col1 > 20
   ```

You can alter read ahead configuration parameters that affect sequential scans (number 1 above). These parameters are:

• RA_PAGES—The number of pages that are read ahead.

• RA_THRESHOLD—The number of pages of the RA_PAGES group that are left to be read by the session before another RA_PAGES is read.

For example, if RA_PAGES is set to four and RA_THRESHOLD is set to one, four pages would be read ahead and put in the buffer pool. After the third page is read by the session (one page left to be read), four more pages would be read ahead and put in the buffer pool. This assures that the read-ahead mechanism is always slightly ahead of the session.

The number of pages read ahead by index scans cannot be directly modified by read-ahead parameters. Instead, they are a function of the number of active sessions and the buffer pool size.

Usually, the default read-ahead parameters should be sufficient. However, if you are doing a great deal of sequential reading (for example, with index builds), you may want to increase the read-ahead values somewhat. If you set the read-ahead parameters too high, the extra pages put in the buffer pool may replace pages of data needed by other sessions, requiring them to perform a disk read instead. You can see evidence of read-aheads set too high if the read cache rate decreases.

In addition to the cache rate, **onstat -p** also shows how many pages are being read ahead.

```
ixda-RA    idx-RA  da-RA   RA-pgsused
2          0       3182    3093
```

The **ixda-RA** column is the number of data pages read ahead because of a sequential read of an index. The **idx-RA** column shows the number of index pages read ahead because of a key-only read operation. The **da-RA** column is the number of pages read ahead in a sequential scan. And **RA-pgsused** is the number of read-ahead pages actually used by the session.

Unfortunately, there is no good way to tell whether you have set the read-ahead parameters sufficiently, other than timing performance of certain activities that read pages sequentially.

4.17 CASE STUDY

The users start to complain about intermittently slow response times during busy times of the day. After monitoring system CPU usage to make sure the system is not overloaded, you decide to check the OnLine system.

The slow response time might be occurring during a checkpoint. Since a checkpoint can stop all critical actions (writing to a page, for example), users might be waiting for a long checkpoint to complete.

You run **tbstat -RF** to determine how many disk writes are occurring during the checkpoint:

```
Fg Writes    LRU Writes    Chunk Writes

0            24879         3773
```

In this example, the bulk of the writes are occurring between checkpoints. However, there is a significant number of Chunk Writes (writes occurring during a checkpoint), so it might be worthwhile to tune the LRU parameters (LRU_MAX_DIRTY and LRU_MIN_DIRTY) to decrease this number.

Also, the checkpoint duration once during the testing cycle was fairly long (25 seconds), as shown in **onstat -m** (note this is an option of version 6.0; in version 5.0, you must physically time the checkpoint duration):

```
16:03:40 Checkpoint Completed: duration was 13 seconds

16:08:28 Checkpoint Completed: duration was 25 seconds

16:13:49 Checkpoint Completed: duration was 7 seconds

16:19:05 Checkpoint Completed: duration was 10 seconds
```

One possible symptom users may see during long checkpoint durations are transactions that seem to "hang" momentarily, waiting for the checkpoint to complete.

To decrease the Chunk writes (writes that occur during checkpoints) and hopefully decrease the checkpoint duration, you decide to decrease LRU_MAX_DIRTY and LRU_MIN_DIRTY. By increasing LRU_MAX_DIRTY to 10 and LRU_MIN_DIRTY to 5, most of the disk writes occur between checkpoints.

The **onstat -RF** output after this change looks like:

```
Fg Writes    LRU Writes    Chunk Writes
0            32551         2632
```

You rerun **onstat -m** and find that the checkpoint duration decreases:

```
17:03:30 Checkpoint Completed: duration was 1 seconds

17:08:18 Checkpoint Completed: duration was 7 seconds

17:13:39 Checkpoint Completed: duration was 7 seconds

17:18:56 Checkpoint Completed: duration was 7 seconds
```

Table 4.1-Disk-tuning checklist

What to Check	How to Check	How to Alter
Read cache rate	tbstat -p (onstat -p)	BUFFERS config. parameter
Write cache rate	tbstat -p (onstat -p)	BUFFERS config. parameter
Checkpoint interval	tbstat -m (onstat -m)	CKPTINTVL config parameter or physical log size
Checkpoint duration	onstat -m (version 6.0 only)	LRU_MAX_DIRTY, LRU_MIN_DIRTY, CKPTINTVL config. parameters or physical log size.
Page cleaning	tbstat -RF	CLEANERS, LRU_MAX_DIRTY, LRU_MIN_DIRTY, LRUS, BUFFERS config parameters
Disk placement	tbstat -D iostat, sar	Change arrangement of items on disk.
Read ahead (version 6.0)	onstat -p	RA_PAGES, RA_THRESHOLD
AIO vps (version 6.0)	onstat -g ioq	NUMAIOVPS

Chapter 5

Memory Performance

This chapter discusses how memory can affect performance of the OnLine system. Memory is a performance factor only if there is not enough of it to do the required work.

The major topics discussed in this chapter are listed below.

- The types of memory to monitor

- Computing memory requirements

- How to monitor memory

- Tips for decreasing the use of memory

5.1   THE TYPES OF MEMORY TO MONITOR

Memory takes one of two forms in an OnLine system: *process memory* and *shared memory*. Process memory refers to the memory needed for database server processes. Shared memory holds information used by all database server processes, such as the buffer cache, the lock and latch structures, and the logical log buffer.

Version 5.0 Memory

In OnLine version 5.0, one database server process (**sqlturbo**) runs for each user. The data portion of memory for each process is dynamic and grows independently as needed for each user. For example, if the user executes a large stored procedure, the code for the stored procedure is brought in to the database server process and put in a cache of stored procedures specifically for reuse by the same user. To determine how much memory the database server processes are using, you should monitor each process during a period of average activity.

73

In addition to the database server processes, there is a master process, called **tbinit**, that coordinates activities such as the initialization of shared memory and checkpoints. The size of this process generally remains static.

There is also a set of page cleaner processes that handle writing pages from memory to disk. These processes are listed by **ps** as **tbpgcl**, or sometimes as **tbinit**, because they are started as child processes to the master **tbinit** process.

Finally, you may see sort processes if you are running parallel sorts.

The amount of shared memory used for OnLine remains static while the OnLine system is up. The size of OnLine shared memory is altered by changing the shared memory configuration parameters. The main determinant of the total size of shared memory is the size of the buffer cache. Figure 5.1 shows the memory requirements for version 5.0

Figure 5.1-   5.0 Memory requirements

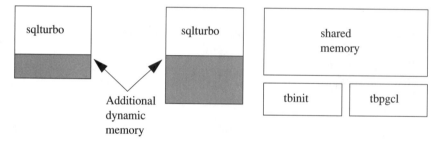

Version 6.0 Memory

In version 6.0, the work of all users is accomplished by a few (approximately 7–20) database server processes since the processes are multithreaded. The database server processes, or *virtual processors* (vps), start when OnLine comes up and stay running until OnLine stops. The **ps** listing shows the virtual processors running as **oninit**. The process sizes of the vps remain static while they are running.

The shared memory requirements for version 6.0 increase dramatically from version 5.0, mainly because shared memory holds much of the data previously held in the **sqlturbo** processes (see Figure 5.2). The OnLine shared memory is divided into three parts:

1.   Resident—This shared memory is very similar to the shared memory in version 5.0. It is static, and contains structures such as the buffer cache, locks, and logical and physical logs.

2. Virtual—This shared memory contains structures needed mainly by the multi-threaded subsystem, such as each user thread's stack. Virtual memory is organized in *pools*, where each pool is used for a specific purpose. Each pool is allocated as needed and released when no longer needed. In version 5.0, much of this memory was kept in each user's database server process. Because the 6.0 multithreaded database server allows a thread to run on multiple processes, the pools must be localized in shared memory so they can be accessed by all virtual processors. The virtual shared memory may grow as needed as users connect and execute SQL statements.

3. Message—This shared memory is used as a bulletin board for messages between the client and database server processes. This shared memory is static and is configurable by setting the maximum number of shared memory connections in the OnLine configuration file.

Figure 5.2- Version 6.0 memory requirements

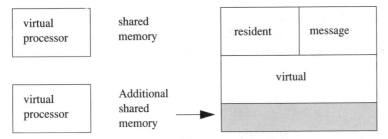

Application Memory

Although application processes are not discussed in detail in this book, it is worth mentioning that you should take application process memory into account when calculating total memory requirements. If applications are running on the same machine as OnLine, they could potentially take up much of the total memory.

5.2 COMPUTING MEMORY REQUIREMENTS

Process Memory

Each process is made up of three parts: the text (or code size), the stack, and the data. Informix database server processes share the same code, or text space, so this amount need be accounted for only once for all occurrences of the same process.

You can use the UNIX **size** command to determine the fixed size of a process (not including any extra memory added as the process is running). For example, to run the **size** command for the **sqlturbo** process (5.0):

```
% size sqlturbo
```

```
text        data    bss      dec       hex
1171456    122880  12640   1306976   13f160
```

In this example, the text size is 1,171,456 bytes, or 1.12 megabytes. The data and stack can be calculated by adding the **data** and **bss** columns. The example shows the data and stack to be 122,880 + 12,640 = 148,160 bytes, or approximately 144 Kbytes.

Since the **sqlturbo** process (in 5.0) grows during its execution, you must monitor the process size during levels of average and peak activity to determine the maximum amount of memory it needs. You can use the UNIX **ps** command to determine the size of the data and stack at any one point in time. Using BSD UNIX, run the following command:

```
ps -aux|grep sqlturbo
```

To determine the current size of the data and stack for the process, examine the SZ column. In the example below, the data and stack size is 180 kilobytes—about 46K more than what was reported with the **size** command.

```
USER  PID   %CPU  %MEM  SZ   RSS TT   STAT   START TIME COMMAND
joe   3097  0.0   0.0   180  0   p3   IW     12:48 0:00sqlturbo
```

Estimating Shared Memory Size: 5.0

In version 5.0, estimating the size of shared memory is easy. The **tbmonitor** tool automatically calculates the approximate size based on the configuration parameters you enter. Choose the **Parameters:Shared Memory** option to get the screen that looks like this:

```
                    SHARED MEMORY PARAMETERS

    Page Size                      [    2] Kbytes

    Server Number                  [    0]    Server Name [ONLINE        ]
    Deadlock Timeout               [   60] Seconds
    Forced Residency               [N]
    Number of Page Cleaners        [    1]

    Physical Log Buffer Size  [     32] Kbytes
    Logical Log Buffer Size   [     32] Kbytes
    Max # of Logical Logs        [    6]
    Max # of Users            [   20]
    Max # of Locks            [ 2000]
    Max # of Buffers          [  200]
    Max # of Chunks              [    8]
    Max # of Open Tblspaces      [  200]
    Max # of Dbspaces            [    8]
                                 =============
    Shared memory size        [      768] Kbytes
```

As you adjust the parameters in brackets that affect the shared memory size, the **Shared memory size** field at the bottom of the screen is recalculated. The configuration parameters that affect the shared memory size are the physical and logical log buffers, the maximum number of users, the maximum number of locks, the maximum number of buffers, the maximum number of chunks, the maximum number of open tablespaces, and the maximum number of dbspaces. The parameter that changes shared memory most significantly is the maximum number of buffers.

You can also see the size of shared memory once OnLine is running with any **tbstat** command. The top part of the output reports the shared memory size in Kbytes. The example below shows an OnLine system that is using approximately 10.3 megabytes.

```
RSAM Version 5.00.UC1D3--On-Line--Up 00:13:10--10552 Kbytes
```

Estimating Shared Memory Size: 6.0

In version 6.0, the resident shared memory segments can be calculated using **onmonitor** through the **Parameters:Shared Memory** menu option. The screen looks like this:

```
                        SHARED MEMORY PARAMETERS
Server Number                      [  6]        Server Name [onlineshm       ]
Server Aliases [                                                             ]
Dbspace Temp   [                                                             ]
Deadlock Timeout                 [  60] Secs  Number of Page Cleaners  [   1]
Forced Residency                   [N]         Stack Size (Kbytes)      [  32]
Non Res. SegSize (Kbytes)   [   8000]

Physical Log Buffer Size  [      32] Kbytes
Logical Log Buffer Size   [      32] Kbytes
Max # of Logical Logs        [   6]          Transaction Timeout      [ 300]
Max # of Transactions     [     60]          Long TX HWM              [  70]
Max # of Userthreads      [     60]          Long TX HWM Exclusive    [  80]
Max # of Locks            [   2000]          Index Page Fill Factor   [  90]
Max # of Buffers          [    400]
Max # of Chunks              [   8]
Max # of Open Tblspaces      [ 200]
Max # of Dbspaces            [   8]
                          =============
Shared memory size        [     1264] Kbytes          Page Size [    2] Kbytes
```

As you adjust the configuration parameters that affect the resident size, you will see the **Shared memory size** field at the bottom of the screen increase. The configuration parameters that affect the resident size are the physical and logical log buffers, the maximum number of user threads, the maximum number of locks, the maximum number of buffers, the maximum number of chunks, the maximum number of open tablespaces, and the maximum number of dbspaces. The parameter that changes the resident portion of shared memory most significantly is the maximum number of buffers.

The message shared memory segments tend to be relatively small and are calculated from the number of shared memory connections specified in the NETTYPE parameter. The NETTYPE parameter has several fields—the third field specifies the number of connections. In the example below, 50 connections are allowed via shared memory:

```
NETTYPE ipcshm,1,50,CPU
```

The formula for calculating the approximate message segment size in bytes is as follows:

```
(10,531 * #connections) + 50,000
```

Using the NETTYPE parameter shown above with 50 connections, the size of the message segment would be (10,531 * 50) + 50,000, or approximately 563 Kbytes.

The size of virtual shared memory segments you need is very difficult to estimate. This is because memory is allocated as needed by individual sessions. If the virtual segments cannot handle the memory needed by a session, another shared memory segment is automatically allocated by OnLine. Shared memory segments are not de-allocated until the OnLine system is brought down.

As a rule of thumb, each session running basic SQL statements will need around 100k of virtual shared memory. However, the following things can really increase the amount of shared memory needed by a session:

• Sorts

• Large stored procedures

• **oncheck** runs

For example, a sort can be anywhere from 100k to 1.5 megabytes, depending on the size of the columns being sorted. If your applications have any SELECT statements with an ORDER BY clause, or if you are creating indexes, you should estimate approximately 500k per session during peak periods.

5.3   HOW TO MONITOR MEMORY

Shared Memory Usage

UNIX allocates memory in units of a segment. How many segments OnLine uses depends upon several things: the UNIX kernel segment size, the amount of memory initially requested by OnLine, and the amount of memory required once the OnLine system is up (6.0 only).

The UNIX kernel segment size is specified by the SHMMAX or SHMSIZE kernel parameter (the parameter name varies from system to system). Suppose the SHMMAX parameter is set at one megabyte, and OnLine requests ten megabytes of shared memory. In this case, ten UNIX shared memory segments are created.

You will want to monitor the number of shared memory segments created as well as the amount of shared memory used. Some operating systems have a limit to the number of segments that can be created. Most operating systems constrain the number of segments by a kernel parameter (SHMMNI).

The UNIX **ipcs** command lists each shared memory segment and its appropriate size.

```
%ipcs -m


IPC status from prod as of Sun Jan 23 13:32:17 1994
T ID KEY              MODE       OWNER     GROUP    SEGSZ
Shared Memory:
m 0 0x52574801 --rw-rw---- informix informix   1048576
m 1 0x52574802 --rw-rw---- informix informix   1048576
m 2 0x52574803 --rw-rw---- informix informix   1048576
m 3 0x52574804 --rw-rw---- informix informix   1048576
m 4 0x52574805 --rw-rw---- informix informix    819200
```

In the above example, five shared memory segments have been allocated with a total of (1,048,576 * 4 + 819,200) = 5,013,504 bytes or 4,816 Kbytes.

In version 6.0, you can identify the type of each segment allocated with the **onstat -g seg** command. A sample output of this command is shown below.

```
Segment Summary:
 (resident segments are not locked)
 id   key          addr    size    ovhd class blkused blkfree
 100  1381779457  800000  2613248 780   R      315      4
 103  1381779460  a7e000  8192000 696   V      288      712
 11   1381779468  124e000 262144  576   M      29       3
```

In the above example, three "segments" are allocated, one for resident shared memory, one for virtual shared memory, and one for messages for shared memory communication. Each is identified as such in the **class** column. For each "segment," you are shown the approximate amount of memory used and the amount of memory free in 8k blocks. This information is only valuable for the virtual segments. If the virtual segments show close to 0 blocks free, you know that another virtual segment will be allocated automatically as soon as a session requests more memory.

Note that the **onstat** output does not show the breakdown of memory by UNIX segment. For example, if OnLine requests 16 megabytes of shared memory and UNIX creates segments of 8 megabytes, then two segments would be created, but only one would be shown in the **onstat** output. To find the exact number of segments created, run the **ipcs** command.

Determining if Memory Usage Is Too High

If there is an insufficient amount of memory in the operating system to handle the work load, UNIX will start *paging*; that is, pages in memory will be written to disk to make way for pages that are needed by running processes. Some paging is normal and acceptable, since there will be some pages in shared memory or in your program that are not needed most of the time. These pages can easily be moved to disk and probably will be, since UNIX uses a least recently used algorithm to decide which pages to move to disk. However, you will experience some performance degradation if UNIX starts to move pages that are needed often by the database server to disk.

In severely memory-starved systems, the operating system will begin to swap entire processes to disk. Any swapping occurring on most systems is very undesirable.

For BSD UNIX systems, the **vmstat** utility is helpful in determining if memory usage is too high. The **po** (page-out) column shows the amount of page-out activity in your system. In the example below, the system is in good shape, as **po** is close to or at 0.

```
procs  memory              page           disk         faults       cpu
 r b w avm fre    re at pi po fr de sr d0 d1 d2 d3 in  sy   cs  us sy id
 1 0 0   28688 0  6  0  1  2  0  0  0  4  2  5  46  254  116 5   2  93
 1 2 0 0 28636 0  0  0  0  0  0  0  0  31 18 31 282 1373 674 27 11 62
 1 3 0 0 28544 0  0  0  0  0  0  0  0  28 16 35 321 1386 699 29 13 58
```

For System V UNIX, the **sar -r** command shows how much free memory is available, and the **sar -p** command shows the number of page faults. If page faults are high, the system is short of memory.

```
sar -r 5 5
    09:18:21 freemem  freeswp
    09:18:26 9902      592384
    09:18:31 9941      592384
    09:18:36 9921      592384
    09:18:41 9922      592384
    09:18:46 9903      592384
    Average  9925      592384
```

```
sar -p 5 5
    09:20:27    vflt/s    pflt/s    pgfil/s    rclm/s
    09:20:32    9.94      0.00      0.00       0.00
    09:20:37    5.17      0.00      0.00 q     0.00
    09:20:42    4.56      0.00      0.00       0.00
    09:20:47    17.17     0.00      0.00       0.00
    09:20:52    4.17      0.00      0.00       0.00
    Average     8.19      0.00      0.00       0.00
```

5.4   SUGGESTIONS TO IMPROVE MEMORY USAGE

There is not much you can do to decrease the memory usage of the database server. It is probably more efficient to just buy more memory. However, given that this might not be possible, there are some things you can do.

The 5.0 Release

1. Decrease the size of the OnLine buffer cache. The biggest effect on shared memory usage is the number of buffers allocated with the BUFFERS configuration parameter. However, by decreasing the buffer cache, you may be impacting performance in another way, by increasing the amount of disk reads and writes.

2. Limit the size of stored procedures. Sixteen of the most recently used stored procedures are cached in **sqlturbo** memory at all times. If stored procedures are large, this could mean that a great deal of memory could be allocated for the cache. By breaking a stored procedure into smaller stored procedures, you can decrease the total memory needed for stored procedures.

3. Limit the size and number of sorts that you run. Although sorts use disks to hold intermediate sorted runs, the current working sort run is held in memory. The administrator does not have direct impact on the size of the sort run held in memory. However, as the size of the value being sorted increases, the size of the sort run increases as well. Unless necessary, you should avoid sorting large character strings. Sorts occur under the following circumstances:

    • SELECT statements using the ORDER BY clause or the GROUP BY clause where an index cannot be used. You can decrease sorting by adding an index on a column that is sorted frequently.

    • SELECT statements that the optimizer chooses to use a sort merge join to join two tables together. This most likely occurs when one or more of the join columns do not have indexes.

• Index builds. The key value is sorted before the index is built. You can bypass the sort routine by setting the NOSORTINDEX environment variable. However, index builds on larger tables will be *much slower* with NOSORTINDEX set.

The 6.0 Release

The 6.0 release allows you to place a cap on the amount of shared memory that is used by the OnLine system. The parameter SHMTOTAL is the total amount of shared memory that can be allocated for an OnLine system. If OnLine tries to allocate another shared memory segment because a session needs more memory and the SHMTOTAL limit is reached, the task for which the session needed memory will fail.

In addition to capping the shared memory used, you can also control how much shared memory is allocated when more memory is required. The SHMVIRTSIZE parameter is the amount of virtual shared memory allocated to the OnLine system when it is brought up. The default value for this parameter is 8,000 Kbytes and will most certainly need to be increased. The SHMADD parameter controls the amount of shared memory that is added when the system is up and more virtual shared memory is required. The default value is 8,000 Kbytes, which means that any time a session needs memory and can't get it from the existing virtual segments, another 8,000 Kbytes will be added. Figure 5.3 illustrates how these configuration parameters affect shared memory.

Figure 5.3-   How configuration parameters affect shared memory

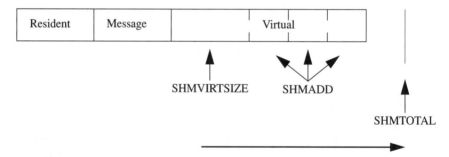

Once these segments have been allocated, they cannot be de-allocated except by bringing down the OnLine system. Note, however, that shared memory pages are treated like any other memory. They can be paged out if real memory is needed for any other purpose. This can hurt performance, though, if the pages being written to swap area are needed by other running processes.

Other than capping the amount of shared memory allocated, here are two suggestions for reducing the amount of memory used by OnLine.

1. Since the biggest users of memory for individual sessions are sorts, you may be able to decrease memory usage by limiting the number of sorts executed simultaneously by sessions.

2. The biggest user of the resident shared memory is the buffer cache. You can change the size of the buffer cache with the BUFFERS configuration parameter. However, by decreasing the buffer cache, you may be impacting performance in another way, by increasing the amount of disk reads and writes.

5.5 MEMORY CALCULATIONS

Tables 5.1 and 5.2 can be used to calculate the memory you will need for your OnLine database server. Some of the values in these worksheets should be obtained by monitoring a running OnLine system.

Table 5.1- Memory Calculation worksheet (5.0)

	TEXT (shared)	(stack/data) (per process)	Shared Memory
sqlturbo processes			
tbinit processes			
shared memory			
Total memory			

Table 5.2- Memory Calculation worksheet (6.0)

	TEXT (shared)	(stack/data) (per process)	Shared Memory
oninit processes			
shared memory			
Total memory			

5.6 CASE STUDY—DETERMINING MEMORY USAGE FOR A 6.0 ONLINE SYSTEM

You manage a 6.0 OnLine system that will be growing by 50 users in the next six months. You need to inform your management now if more memory is required for the added users.

You start by examining the current usage of the OnLine system. The **onstat -g seg** command shows the following shared memory, which has been allocated and represents the maximum amount required since the OnLine system was started:

```
onstat -g seg


id      key            addr       size        ovhd class blkused blkfree

769     1381451777     800000     42000384 1432      R      5123    4
770     1381451778     300e000    61440000 1520      V      7442    58
771     1381451779     6aa6000    311296    588      M      35      3
516     1381451780     6af2000    16777216 836       V      1950    98
517     1381451781     7af2000    16777216 836       V      753     1295
```

From this output, you add up the entries in the size field to get 133,814 Kbytes or 130 megabytes. This number represents the amount of shared memory that has been allocated for the database server. Note that although 130 megabytes has been allocated, the memory not currently used is paged out to disk.

To find out how much shared memory is actually allocated to session and overhead tasks, you add up the entries in the **blkused** column and multiply by 8 to get the approximate number of Kbytes currently used, 122,424. This value is the representation of the total amount of shared memory needed on average by sessions that are currently running. You may run **onstat -g seg** and perform this calculation several times during the day to get a more representative sample of the amount of shared memory that is used at different times.

Next, you determine the size of the **oninit** processes from the **ps** command.

```
USER PID    %CPU   %MEM   SZ    RSS      TT    STAT START   TIME     COMMAND
root 22848 82.1   34.2   320   126948   p2    R     May 9   1385:24 oninit
root 22851 59.1   33.2   308   123112   p2    R     May 9   1009:57 oninit
root 22850 56.3   33.0   308   122704   p2    R     May 9    935:12 oninit
root 22849 0.0    0.3    296   1272     p2    S     May 9      3:43 oninit
root 22853 0.0    0.1    372   352      p2    S     May 9      6:36 oninit
root 22855 0.0    0.4    308   1432     p2    S     May 9      2:50 oninit
root 22852 0.0    0.4    308   1444     p2    S     May 9      2:53 oninit
root 22854 0.0    0.6    320   2396     p2    S     May 9      3:06 oninit
```

The data and stack size of each **oninit** process is approximately 320 Kbytes. For eight oninit processes, the data and stack size used is 320 * 8 = 2,560 Kbytes.

By running a **size** command on the **oninit** process, you measure the size of the text portion of the process.

```
%size $INFORMIXDIR/bin/oninit

text      data    bss     dec      hex

2482176   237568  27552   2747296  29eba0
```

The text size is 2,482,176 bytes, or 2,424 Kbytes.

From these two reports, you can now fill out the current memory calculation worksheet.

	TEXT (shared)	(stack/data) (per process)	Shared Memory
oninit processes	2424 Kbytes	320 Kbytes	
shared memory			122424 Kbytes
Total memory	2424 Kbytes	2560 Kbytes	122424 Kbytes

The total amount of memory currently used is 2,424 + 2,560 + 122,424 = 127,408 Kbytes, or approximately 124 megabytes of memory.

Now you must determine how much memory the average user is allocating. The **onstat -g ses** command lists every active session. From the output of these commands, you record a few session ids and run the following command for each **session_id**:

```
onstat -g ses session_id
```

The output of this command lists, among other things, the shared memory pools that are currently allocated for the session. The output for some sessions looks like:

```
Memory pools count 2

name          class   addr     totalsize freesize  #allocfrag #freefrag

2117          V       35fa010 262144    48908     295        53

2117_SORT_0   V       3694010 352256    42044     7          6
```

This session is currently running a sort, as you notice from the SORT pool that is allocated. The total amount of memory for pools this session currently has allocated is 262,144 + 352,256 = 614,400 bytes, or 600 Kbytes.

```
Memory pools count 1

name          class   addr     totalsize freesize #allocfrag #freefrag

2981          V       5fa2010 32768     5280      78         10
```

This session is using only 32,768 bytes, or 32 Kbytes.

```
Memory pools count 2
name          class   addr      totalsize freesize #allocfrag #freefrag
2810          V       574e010   253952    47044     296        53
2810_SORT_0   V       3f40010   303104    28748     7
```

This session has allocated 253,952 + 303,104 bytes, or 544 Kbytes.

After examining the output from other sessions at different times of the day, you conclude that 500 Kbytes per user is not unreasonable during peak periods of the day. For 50 new sessions running similar applications as the currently running sessions, you will need 50 * 500 Kbytes, or approximately an additional 25 megabytes of memory during peak periods.

Chapter 6

CPU Usage and Performance

This chapter discusses how CPU usage affects database server performance and how the database server can be tuned to take full advantage of multiprocessor systems.

The major topics discussed in this chapter are listed below.

• Informix and multiprocessor systems

• How to monitor CPU usage

• What to expect in performance improvements by adding more processors

• How to tune processor usage in version 5.0

• How to tune processor usage in version 6.0

6.1 INFORMIX AND MULTIPROCESSOR SYSTEMS

INFORMIX-OnLine and INFORMIX-OnLine Dynamic Server can run on single-processor systems, or on a special class of multiprocessor systems called symmetrical multiprocessing (SMP) systems. In an SMP system, processors are executing independent code, but must communicate with other processors from time to time. A high-speed bus is used to connect all processors to each other and to a common set of memory. The number of processors that can effectively be used in a system depends heavily on the amount of traffic between processors that the bus can handle.

Parallel processing means that a task is split into pieces and processed in parallel. Informix accomplishes parallel processing in version 6.0 by spreading tasks across processes, which in turn may be run on different processors in an SMP system. OnLine will act as a "scheduler" to assign threads to virtual processors. However, it is the responsibility of the UNIX scheduler to assign the virtual processors (which are simply processes) to a hardware processor.

6.2 HOW TO MONITOR CPU USAGE

On BSD UNIX systems, you can monitor the overall usage of the CPU with the **vmstat** command. An example output looks something like this:

```
procs memory              page            disk        faults       cpu
r b w avm fre    re at pi po fr de sr d0 d1 d2 d3 in  sy   cs  us sy id
1 0 0 0  28688   0  6  0  1  2  0  0  0  4  2  5 46  254  116  5  2 93
1 2 0 0  28636   0  0  0  0  0  0  0  0 31 18 31 282 1373 674 27 11 62
1 3 0 0  28544   0  0  0  0  0  0  0  0 28 16 35 321 1386 699 29 13 58
```

The columns that report information about CPU activity are the last three columns:

- The **us** column shows the percentage of the time the CPU was executing processes in the user state.
- The **sy** column shows the percentage of time the CPU was executing processes in the system state (kernel activity and other system overhead).
- The **id** column shows the percentage of time the CPU was idle.

The system in the example is in good shape, with 62% and 58% of the CPU idle during the sample time.

Another important piece of information is the first column, which displays the run queue. The run queue statistic is a count of the number of processes that are ready to run but are waiting, usually for CPU availability.

You can see System V UNIX processor activity with **sar -u**.

```
00:00:00 %usr   %sys %wio   %idle
01:00:01 20     9    2      69
02:00:01 22     8    3      67
03:00:01 25     9    2      64
```

If the **%wio** value is significant in this output, your system may actually be I/O-bound, even if the **%idle** is low. You should investigate your disk performance in this case.

The System V command to monitor the run queue is **sar -q**.

For multiprocessor systems, it is helpful to view the activity of individual processors. Most multiprocessor systems have utilities to do this. For example, the multiprocessor SUN Microsystems machines have the **mpstat** utility, which gives the CPU utilization by processor.

```
average       cpu0         cpu1         cpu2         cpu3
us ni sy id us ni sy id us ni sy id us ni sy id us ni sy id
38 0  14 48 37 0  14 48 37 0  14 48 37 0  14 48 38 0  14 48
69 0  11 20 83 0  11  6 77 0  11 12 53 0  10 37 64 0  12 24
64 0  20 16 57 0  19 24 75 0  19  6 64 0  15 21 60 0  26 14
```

6.3   WILL ADDING ANOTHER PROCESSOR HELP PERFORMANCE?

Version 5.0

In version 5.0 of OnLine, most of the work for one user is done within one process, the **sqlturbo** process. Consider a program, running by itself on a system, which performs an UPDATE statement to update one million rows into a table, using the **sqlturbo** process to perform each of the inserts serially. Even though the **sqlturbo** process can migrate from one processor to another on a multiprocessor system, it is only running on one processor at a time. This means that the UPDATE statement for one user does not take advantage of multiple hardware processors. In fact, an UPDATE statement running by itself on a machine generally *will not run faster* on a multiprocessor machine than it will on a single-processor machine. This is a common mistake in thinking for administrators planning to upgrade their machine to a multiprocessor variety. Generally, it is the speed of the individual processor that will determine the speed of any individual database activity.

Now consider an OnLine system with100 active users, each with its own **sqlturbo** process. If a single CPU system is showing 100% usage with 100 users, and the system run queue is consistently high, moving to a multiprocessor architecture or a single-processor system with a faster CPU will probably show performance improvements. With a multiprocessor system, each CPU can run an **sqlturbo** process simultaneously. Figure 6.1 illustrates the relationship between hardware processors and database server processes in version 5.0.

Figure 6.1-   Hardware processor to database server process relationship (5.0)

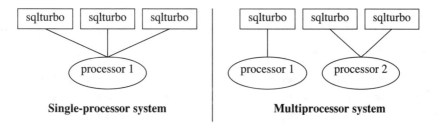

Single-processor system | **Multiprocessor system**

Does this mean that, if one CPU is at 100% capacity, that doubling the number of processors will double performance? At some point while adding additional processors, other system bottlenecks (disk, memory, etc.) will prevent the system from using all of every processor for meaningful work.

Version 6.0

The 6.0 release is designed to work more efficiently with multiprocessor machines running many users. The CPU virtual processors do most of the CPU-intensive work for multiple users or sessions (see Figure 6.2).

Figure 6.2-   Hardware processor to database server process relationship (6.0)

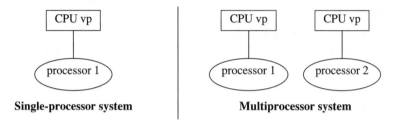

With the 6.0 multithreaded architecture, each session can have multiple threads. Each thread can run on a separate CPU vp, effectively parallelizing an individual user's activity. In reality, the 6.0 release only spawns multiple threads for the following activities:

• Sorting

• Index builds

• Database restores

Parallel activities should run faster as you add more processors (and CPU vps). Each thread can run on different CPU vps, and each CPU vp can run on a different processor. This means that one session's sorting or CREATE INDEX statement can run on multiple processors at once (see Figure 6.3).

However, for all other operations, a session's activity will only run as fast as it could on a single-processor system, similar to the 5.0 release. However, in later releases of the OnLine Dynamic Server, multiple threads will be spawned for database queries, effectively parallelizing the SELECT statement for one session.

For version 6.0 database servers, a processor overload may be evident only by the CPU idle time. The run queue of a system with a 6.0 OnLine system may be close to zero, because the CPU vps are the only processes within the OnLine system with heavy processor usage.

Figure 6.3- How multithreading can parallelize an activity (6.0)

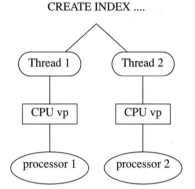

6.4 HOW TO INFLUENCE PROCESSOR USAGE IN 5.0

Beyond adding processors if you are CPU-bound, there are a few things you can do to affect the amount of processor usage:

1. Move the application processes off the database server machine. Although there are inherent network delays added when you move the client applications to another machine, these network delays may be better than having an overloaded processor on the system running the database server.

2. Modify the SPINCNT configuration parameter. When a database server process is waiting for another database server process to release a latch (an internal lock), it can do one of two things: sleep, or keep trying to obtain the latch. Putting a process to sleep requires a small amount of overhead, but is the appropriate thing to do on single-processor machines. However, with a multiprocessor system, it might make sense to avoid the expensive operation of putting the process to sleep and waking it up when the latch is available. When a database server process tries to obtain a latch, it runs in a loop, trying to obtain the latch every x iterations of the loop. As you can imagine, this can use up a significant amount of the processor if many database server processes are doing the same kind of waiting. You can determine the number of times the sqlturbo process tries for the latch by tuning the SPINCNT parameter. For example, by setting SPINCNT to 300, the database server tries to obtain the latch 300 times before giving up and going to sleep. If your CPU usage is high, you may want to decrease the SPINCNT parameter (the default is 300). By setting SPINCNT to zero, the process immediately goes to sleep on a latch wait. If you are using a single-processor machine, make sure SPINCNT is set to zero.

3.   Modify use of parallel sorting. Multiprocessor systems usually benefit from using the parallel sorting feature. In 5.0, this means that multiple sort processes are started to handle a single user's sort request. The sort processes can run in parallel, taking advantage of multiple processors. However, if the CPU idle time is relatively low on all processors, parallel sorting may slow down everything else running on a system.

To sort in parallel, you must set the environment variable PSORT_NPROCS before starting the client application process that will request the sort activity. PSORT_NPROCS should be set to the number of processes that will perform the sort. Generally, you should set PSORT_NPROCS to the number of processors in your system unless the hardware processors show a low %idle with **sar** or **vmstat**.

6.5   HOW TO INFLUENCE PROCESSOR USAGE IN 6.0.

Fortunately, you have more control over processor usage in the 6.0 release. There are several tunable parameters that affect how much processor is used for the database server.

The OnLine process that uses the most "user-state" processor time is the CPU vp. The AIO vp uses some processor time, but it is mostly "system-state" time.

The major tunable parameter that affects processor usage is the number of CPU virtual processors, set by the NUMCPUVPS configuration parameter. The CPU vp does most of the CPU-intensive work of the OnLine system. Generally, you should not have more than one CPU vp per processor. Having more than one per processor requires an increased number of operating system context switches, as the processor must service both processes. If other non-database processing occurs on the same machine, you may want to have significantly fewer CPU vps than hardware processors.

The best way to determine if you have enough CPU vps is to check the size of the OnLine ready queue. The OnLine ready queue (not to be confused with the system ready queue) is a list of all threads that are ready to run but lack a virtual processor to run on. Generally, you would like to see an empty or near-empty ready queue most of the time. You can see the number of ready threads by running **onstat -g rea**. A sample output looks like this:

```
Ready threads:
tid tcb     rstcb  prty status vp-class name

13   b53120  0     2    ready  1cpu  sm_discon
14   b5aed8 8067c4 2    ready  1cpu  flush_sub(0)
44   ca09a4 809dc4 2    ready  1cpu  sqlexec
45   ca946c 809a64 2    ready  1cpu  sqlexec
46   cb69a4 809704 2    ready  1cpu  sqlexec
```

In the above example, three user threads and two system threads are waiting for a free CPU vp to continue work.

If you are running on a single-processor machine, there is not much you can do about a ready queue that constantly has entries. On a multiprocessor machine, you can increase the number of CPU vps by one (until you reach the number of processors on your system) and continue monitoring the ready queue to see if the added processors helped. At some point, however, if CPU utilization for all processors is between 80% and 100%, adding another CPU vp can actually hurt performance.

To add a CPU vp dynamically, run the following command:

```
onmode -p +1 cpu
```

To drop a CPU vp dynamically, run the following command:

```
onmode -p -1 cpu
```

Adding or dropping a CPU vp dynamically does not change the number of CPU vps that will be started the next time the OnLine system comes up. Once you have determined an optimal number of CPU vps to start, modify the NUMCPUVPS configuration parameter or change the value in the **Parameters:perFormance** menu option of **onmonitor**.

Other Considerations

Other than altering the number of CPU vps, there are a few other considerations to improve performance in a version 6.0 system:

1. Set the MULTIPROCESSOR configuration parameter to 1 for multiprocessor machines. This parameter primarily alters the OnLine system to use spin locks for threads. Thread spin locks keep threads from being put on a sleep or wait queue while waiting a very short time for a resource. Single-processor systems should set this parameter to 0.

2. Set the SINGLE_CPU_VP parameter to 1 for single-processor systems. This constrains the OnLine system to use only one CPU vp, and turns off some internal locking mechanisms because there is no contention for some resources by two CPU vps. The lack of these internal locks has such a positive effect on performance that even two processor systems may perform better with this parameter set to 1. However, this means that only one CPU vp can be started. For systems with more than two processors, set SINGLE_CPU_VP to 0.

3. Use parallel sorting. Multiprocessor systems usually benefit from using the parallel sorting feature. In version 6.0, this means that multiple sort threads handle a single user's sort request. The sort threads can run in parallel, taking advantage of multiple processors. However, on a highly loaded system, parallel sorting may slow down other operations, because the sort threads will be scheduled on the same CPU vps as

the main session threads that perform other operations. If the OnLine ready queue is constantly loaded (**onstat -g rea**), turning off parallel sorting may help performance. Parallel sorting is turned on by a session if the PSORT_NPROCS environment variable is set.

4. Adjust processor affinity. Processor affinity allows a process to be bound to a single processor. By keeping a process on a processor, you take advantage of processor cache and forgo the overhead required to move a process from one hardware processor to another. Generally, you will want to set affinity on only CPU vps, since they perform the bulk of the work. OnLine has two configuration parameters that turn on processor affinity for systems that support it: AFF_NPROCS and AFF_SPROC. AFF_NPROCS specifies the number of hardware processors to which to assign CPU vps. For example, if AFF_NPROCS is 2, then two processors would run all CPU vps. Generally, you should set AFF_NPROCS to the number of CPU vps in the OnLine system and to a number less than the total number of hardware processors. The AFF_SPROC configuration parameter specifies the starting processor number for affinity (starting at 0). This allows you to pick certain processors to which to assign CPU vps (see Figure 6.4).

Figure 6.4-   Processor affinity example

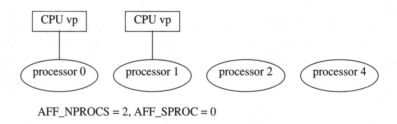

AFF_NPROCS = 2, AFF_SPROC = 0

The number of hardware platforms that support the AFF_NPROCS and AFF_SPROC configuration parameters is limited (check your Informix release notes). However, some operating systems support some kind of processor affinity command that you can use instead of these parameters to achieve the same affect.

6.6 PROCESSOR USAGE CHECKLIST

Table 6.1-Processor Usage Checklist

What to Check	How to Check	How to Alter
SPINCNT (5.0)	Check for %idle of processors with vmstat, sar. Single CPU machines should have SPINCNT set to zero.	SPINCNT configuration parameter.
Parallel sorting (for multiprocessor systems)	Check for %idle of processors with vmstat, sar. Check OnLine ready queue (6.0) with onstat -g rea	Set (or unset) the PSORT_NPROCS environment variable.
CPU vps (6.0)	onstat -g rea	Increase dynamically by onmode -p. Or change NUMCPUVPS configuration parameter.
MULTIPROCESSOR configuration parameter (6.0)	$ONCONFIG file	Turn on (1) for multiprocessor machines. Turn off (0) for single-processor machines.
SINGLE_CPU_VP (6.0)	$ONCONFIG file	Turn on (1) for single-processor machines. Turn off (0) for multiprocessor machines.
Processor Affinity (6.0)		AFF_NPROCS, AFF_SPROC, or by an operating system command.

Chapter 7

Query Performance

This chapter discusses techniques a database administrator may employ to improve query performance.

The major topics discussed in this chapter are listed below.

• How the query optimizer works

• How indexes affect the optimizer

• What statistics are kept by the optimizer

• When the statistics are updated

• Viewing the query path

• How to influence the optimizer

7.1 HOW THE QUERY OPTIMIZER WORKS

The query optimizer is responsible for determining the best way to perform a specific query. It is generally *cost-based*, meaning the optimizer computes a cost for each *query path* and chooses the lowest cost path. A query path is simply a distinct method of executing a query that takes into account the order in which tables are read, how they are read (by an index or sequentially), and how they are joined with other tables in the query.

Join Methods

Before discussing the query optimizer further, it is important to understand how a query with more than one table can be executed. To join two tables, the database server must find a row that meets the query criteria in the first table and join it with the second

97

table. The join consists of determining if a row in the second table meets the join filter criteria as well as other criteria in the query. For example, consider the following SELECT statement:

```
select * from customer,contact

    where customer.customer_num = contact.customer_num

        and customer.customer_num = 3020
```

The join filter between the two tables in the example is **customer.customer_num = contact.customer_num**. A row must be found in each table that has the same **customer_num** value. OnLine has a few choices in how the join between two tables is accomplished:

- Nested loop join—The nested loop join is a method where the first table is scanned for rows that meet the query criteria. Once a row is found in the first table, the database server searches for a corresponding row in the second table. Without indexes, the server would have to scan the first table once, and the second table x times where x is the number of rows that meet the query criteria in the first table. Luckily, the optimizer usually chooses this method only if the second table has an index on the join column, so the entire second table does not have to be scanned once for each row found in the first table.

- Sort merge join—This join method is usually used when no index is available on the join column for both tables. Before the join begins, the database server sorts the rows from each table (after applying any query filters) on the join column. Once the rows are sorted, the algorithm for joining the two tables is easy. The database server simply reads both sorted tables sequentially.

- Hash join—The hash join is a join method that was added in the INFORMIX-OnLine Dynamic Server in version 7.0. It is used when there are no indexes in one or both of the tables in the join and will usually replace the use of the sort merge join. One table is scanned and used to create a hash table. Using an internal hash function, each row is put in a "bucket" with other rows that have the same hash value. Once the first table has been scanned and placed in a hash table, the second table is scanned once, and each row is looked up in the hash table to see if a join can be made. A hash join is usually faster than a sort merge join because no sort is required. However, there is some overhead in creating the hash table.

When join columns for both tables are indexed, the SELECT statement will most likely use the nested loop join. The sort merge join has a high overhead in that rows from each table (or each table without an index) must be sorted. However, the sort merge join is preferable when join columns for both tables are not indexed.

Optimizer Paths

Consider the following query:

```
select * from x,y,z where x.a = y.a and y.a = z.a
   and z.b = 30
```

The query would most likely be accomplished by one of the following methods (although all paths are examined!):

1. Choose a row from table x. Then join the row with one or more rows in table y. Join the result with table z.

2. Choose a row from table y. Then join the row with one or more rows in table x. Join the result with table z. (See Figure 7.1.)

3. Choose a row from table z. Then join the row with one or more rows in table y. Join the result with table x.

Figure 7.1-   How tables are joined: an example.

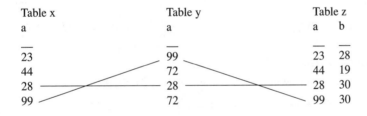

The order and the method in which the tables are read make up the query path. In determining the query path, the optimizer will try to eliminate as many rows as possible early in the query. The smaller the number of rows that will fulfill the query from each table, the higher the probability that the table will be towards the front of the path. The number of rows that will fulfill the query for a table is known as the *table selectivity*. In the example, table z is probably the most selective because of the filter **z.b = 30**. Assuming the tables are of equal size and **z.b** has an index, the optimizer will most likely choose the zyx path (path number three).

Note that the order of the tables in the query path is very important. For example, examining table **x** first and joining it with table **y** may be much better than examining table **y** first and joining it with table **x**.

7.2   INDEXES AND THE OPTIMIZER

The presence of indexes on filter columns in a SELECT statement profoundly affect the optimizer path and, eventually, the performance of a query. It would be wonderful to have an index on every column used as a filter in a query. However, the reality is that indexes take up disk space and adversely affect performance for INSERT, UPDATE, and DELETE statements. The administrator must balance decision support needs with OLTP needs in deciding which columns to index.

As a minimum, you should index all primary and foreign keys in a database. Additionally, any columns that are used in important queries can be indexed as required.

7.3   OPTIMIZER STATISTICS

The optimizer uses statistics kept for a table to determine the selectivity. These statistics are kept in a series of system catalog tables (which are simply control tables kept with each database). The statistics kept for a table and its indexes are listed below.

- **systables.nrows**: number of rows in the table
- **systables.npused**: number of pages used to store the data
- **syscolumns.colmax**: second largest value for a column (discarding the maximum value)
- **syscolumns.colmin**: second smallest value for a column (discarding the minimum value)
- **sysindexes.leaves**: number of leaf pages for the index
- **sysindexes.nunique**: number of unique values for the first column in the index
- **sysindexes.clust**: how highly clustered the values for the first column in the index are

Here's a simple example of how these statistics are used by the optimizer.

```
    select * from customer where city = "LOS ANGELES"
and
        customer_name = "ALVAREZ"
```

If the customer table has an index on both **city** and **customer_name**, which index should be used? Suppose the table has the following statistics:

```
    systables.nrows = 1,000,000
    sysindexes.nunique (for customer_name index) =
200000
    sysindexes.nunique (for city index) = 100
```

Using these statistics, the optimizer can guess that there might be approximately 1,000,000/200,000 = 5 occurrences of "ALVAREZ" in the table and 1,000,000/100 = 100,000 customers that live in "LOS ANGELES" in the table. Given this simple calculation, the optimizer would most likely choose the **customer_name** index to retrieve the data. In reality, there are other statistics that the optimizer would analyze as well, such as the number of pages in each index and the number of levels of each b-tree.

The importance of these statistics is magnified when three or more tables are involved in a query.

Note that the optimizer cannot discern if the data within a table is skewed. Also, there is no information on unique values for columns that are not indexed (this deficiency is addressed in the 6.0 data distributions feature addressed later in this chapter).

7.4 WHEN ARE THE STATISTICS UPDATED?

The statistics in the system catalog tables are not constantly updated. This type of behavior would be too costly to overall performance. Instead, the UPDATE STATISTICS statement refreshes the system catalog table statistics. You decide how often to run the UPDATE STATISTICS statement.

A disadvantage of running the UPDATE STATISTICS statement frequently is that it does incur some overhead because all index and data pages must be read to calculate the statistics. Since the pages are read into the buffer cache, you may see the overall read cache rate decrease while UPDATE STATISTICS is running. Also, when the statistics have been calculated, OnLine must briefly lock some rows in the system catalog tables to update the statistics. At the brief moment these columns are locked, other SQL statements needing to read these rows will receive errors.

It is very important to run UPDATE STATISTICS when the nature of the data in a table has changed significantly, especially after an initial load of data, or after a DELETE or UPDATE that affects a large number of rows. You can update the statistics for one table.

```
UPDATE STATISTICS FOR table
```
You can update the statistics for an entire database.

```
UPDATE STATISTICS
```
You may consider embedding UPDATE STATISTICS in an application process that runs nightly or weekly in a period of slow activity.

7.5 VIEWING THE QUERY PATH

You can record the path the optimizer chooses for a query by running SET EXPLAIN ON before the query is optimized. SET EXPLAIN ON places the query plan in a file in your current directory, called **sqexplain.out**. A sample query plan is listed below.

```
QUERY:
------
select * from orders, items where orders.order_num =
items.order_num

Estimated Cost: 11
Estimated # of Rows Returned: 67


1) informix.orders: SEQUENTIAL SCAN

2) informix.items: INDEX PATH

 (1) Index Keys: order_num
  Lower Index Filter: informix.items.order_num = infor-
mix.orders.order_num
```

The query plan output is valuable for determining if the query is running optimally. Some of the things you can notice about the query plan output are:

- The estimated cost of a query. This value is to compare how "expensive" one path is compared to another. The estimated cost cannot really translate to the amount of time the query will take.

- The estimated number of rows returned by a query. This value will tend to be a very rough estimate, and will be more accurate if all filter columns have indexes and if data distributions (a 6.0 feature explained later in this chapter) were created on all filter columns.

- The order of the tables in the query plan. In the example, the **orders** table is read first, followed by the items table. Ideally, the optimizer chooses the table with the fewest number of rows that will be fulfilled by the query.

- How each table will be read. In the example, the **orders** table will be read sequentially and an index path used for **items**. This is the usual method for a nested loop join when the first table has no filter.

- What indexes will be used for an index scan.

- The type of join method used. If the query path does not mention the join method, the nested loop join will be used. If the sort merge join will be used, you will see something like:

```
   1) informix.items: SEQUENTIAL SCAN

   SORT SCAN: informix.items.order_num
```

```
2) informix.orders: SEQUENTIAL SCAN

SORT SCAN: informix.orders.order_num

MERGE JOIN
      Merge Filters: informix.orders.order_num =
                            informix.items.order_num
```

7.6   CASE STUDY 1

A user complains about the response time of a query. After getting the details about the query, you run and time the query yourself. It takes two minutes to run.

You turn SET EXPLAIN ON and run the query with the parameters the user was running with. The SET EXPLAIN OUTPUT is:

```
QUERY:
------
select * from account,transaction,teller
where account.account_nbr = transaction.account_nbr
and transaction.teller_num = teller.teller_num
and teller.teller_num = 22

Estimated Cost: 46054
Estimated # of Rows Returned: 209

1) informix.transaction: SEQUENTIAL SCAN

2) informix.teller: INDEX PATH
      Filters: informix.teller.teller_num = 22

      (1) Index Keys: teller_num
          Lower Index Filter: informix.teller.teller_num
= informix.transaction.teller_num

3) informix.account: INDEX PATH

      (1) Index Keys: account_nbr
          Lower Index Filter: informix.account.account_nbr
= informix.transaction.account_nbr
```

By looking at the SET EXPLAIN output, you notice the sequential scan of the trans-action table. This operation is probably what is taking the majority of the two minutes to run the query.

You use DB-Access to find the number of rows in each table. The **account** and **transaction** table has approximately the same number of rows: about 30,000. The **teller** table has only 100 entries. By running a few quick SELECT statements, you note that the teller table has only one row where **teller_num = 22**. The **transaction** table is first in the query path because it does not have an index on **teller_num**. By putting the **transaction** table first in the query path, the optimizer avoids putting an index on **teller_num** or using a sort merge to join the **teller** and **transaction** tables.

After some thought about the consequences, you decide to put an index on **transaction.teller_num**. By adding another index, you realize that the INSERT, UPDATE, and DELETE operations on the transaction table may suffer slightly.

After adding the index, the query now runs in five seconds. The SET EXPLAIN output is:

```
QUERY:
------
select * from account,transaction,teller
where account.account_nbr = transaction.account_nbr
and transaction.teller_num = teller.teller_num
and teller.teller_num = 22

Estimated Cost: 111
Estimated # of Rows Returned: 10

1) informix.teller: INDEX PATH

  (1) Index Keys: teller_num
  Lower Index Filter: informix.teller.teller_num = 22

2) informix.transaction: INDEX PATH

  (1) Index Keys: branch_nbr
  Lower Index Filter: informix.transaction.teller_num =
informix.teller.teller_num

3) informix.account: INDEX PATH
```

```
(1) Index Keys: account_nbr
Lower Index Filter: informix.account.account_nbr =
informix.transaction.account_nbr
```

You notice now that the **teller** table is first in the query path, because it is the smaller table and can be joined with **transaction** using an index.

7.7   INFLUENCING THE OPTIMIZER WITH SET OPTIMIZATION LOW

The thoroughness of the optimizer in examining all paths can actually increase the total amount of time the query takes. The optimization time is insignificant for queries involving only a few tables. However, for SELECT statements with more than four or five tables, the number of paths the optimizer must examine increase dramatically, along with the optimization time.

The SET OPTIMIZATION LOW statement, executed before the SELECT statement is optimized, reduces some of the work the optimizer does by eliminating unlikely paths.

Let's use a SELECT statement with four tables as an example of how SET OPTIMIZATION LOW reduces optimization work:

```
select * from w,x,y,z where x.a = y.a and y.b = z.b
    and x.b = w.b
```

First, the optimizer computes a cost for all two-way joins in the query, such as the xy join, the yz join, the xw join, the zy join (order is important!), and so on. The two-way join with the lowest cost is kept, and all other further paths involving the other two-way joins are discarded by the optimizer. For example, if the yz join is the lowest cost, the optimizer would only examine costs for the possible three-way joins that start with the yz join (i.e., yzx and yzw). See Figure 7.2.

The advantages of SET OPTIMIZATION LOW is that the optimization process will run faster for a query involving more than a few tables, because of the vastly reduced number of paths that must be examined. The disadvantage is that the optimizer might inadvertently discard the lowest-cost path early in the analysis, causing the overall query performance to decrease! That is why you should use SET OPTIMIZATION LOW with care.

Here are some guidelines for deciding when to use SET OPTIMIZATION LOW:

1. Only consider using SET OPTIMIZATION LOW if the query has more than four tables.

2. Run and time the query using production data.

3. Obtain the query path by running the query with SET EXPLAIN ON.

4. Obtain the query path by running the query with SET OPTIMIZATION LOW and SET EXPLAIN ON. Is the query path the same as in step 3? If so, then the optimizer chose the correct path while keeping optimization time to a minimum. Continue to step 5.

5. Rerun and time the query using SET OPTIMIZATION LOW. If the query time is significantly faster, then SET OPTIMIZATION LOW will positively affect your performance!

To use SET OPTIMIZATION LOW for a specific query, place the SET OPTIMIZA-TION LOW statement immediately before the query, and SET OPTIMIZATION HIGH after the query. The SET OPTIMIZATION HIGH statement instructs the optimizer to perform a full cost analysis (the default) for queries following. For example:

```
SET OPTIMIZATION LOW
SELECT * FROM ......
SET OPTIMIZATION HIGH
```

Figure 7.2- Optimizer paths with SET OPTIMIZATION LOW

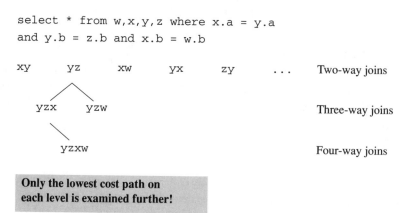

7.8 INFLUENCING THE OPTIMIZER WITH DATA DISTRIBUTIONS (VERSION 6.0 ONLY)

The statistics in **systables, syscolumns,** or **sysindexes** do not take into account any skewed data in the table. In the example SELECT statement used earlier:

```
select * from customer where city = "LOS ANGELES" and
        customer_name = "ALVAREZ"
```

How would the query optimizer know if the **customer** table only held one customer from the city of Los Angeles? Would the optimizer be able to discern that most of the customers in the **customer** table live in Los Angeles?

The effect of skewed data on an optimizer's ability to pick the correct query path will be magnified as more and larger tables are involved in a query.

The 6.0 optimizer uses *data distributions* to detect skewed data and also to provide more information on nonindexed columns.

A distribution can be created on each column. To create a distribution, the table is divided into pieces, or "bins." Each of the bins describe an approximately equal number of rows except for the last bin, which might describe fewer rows than the other bins. Then statistics are gathered and stored for each of these bins. The following information is known for each bin:

- The first and last value represented by the bin
- The number of unique values in each bin
- For the last bin, the number of rows represented by the bin

In addition to statistics kept on each of the bins, information is also kept on any value with a large number of duplicates. To qualify as "highly duplicate," the value must have more duplicates than one-fourth the number of rows in a bin. The highly duplicate values are excluded from the statistics in the individual bins. For each highly duplicate value, the following information is kept:

- The highly duplicate column value
- The number of rows containing the column value

The statistics kept for each bin and for the duplicate are stored, encoded, in a system catalog table, called **sysdistrib**.

Generating a Distribution

To generate a distribution for a column, use the UPDATE STATISTICS statement. You can run the statement for every column in the database, for every column in a table, or for an individual column in a table. You can also choose to sample rows or create a distribution on all of the actual rows. Sampling rows for a distribution is called MEDIUM mode. Using all rows in the table for the distribution is called HIGH mode.

Some examples are shown below.

1.   Create a distribution on a column using sampling (MEDIUM).

```
UPDATE STATISTICS MEDIUM FOR TABLE table(column)
```

2.   Create a distribution on all columns in a table using actual rows (HIGH).

     ```
     UPDATE STATISTICS HIGH FOR TABLE table
     ```

3.   Create a distribution on all columns in a database using sampling.

     ```
     UPDATE STATISTICS MEDIUM
     ```

Displaying a Column Distribution

You can see a column's distribution with the **dbschema** utility, using the **-hd** option.

```
dbschema -d database -hd table
```

A portion of the output of dbschema for one column's distribution is shown below.

```
Distribution for informix.transaction.account_nbr

Constructed on 05/22/1994

High Mode, 0.500000 Resolution


--- DISTRIBUTION ---

 ( 1)
 1: ( 460,  75,  75)
 2: ( 460,  76, 151)
 3: ( 460,  74, 226)
 4: ( 460,  76, 302)
 5: ( 460,  79, 381)
 6: ( 460,  71, 452)
 7: ( 460,  74, 526)
 8: ( 460,  73, 599)
 9: ( 460,  78, 677)
10: ( 460,  79, 757)
```

The statistics for each bin are shown on one line. The first column shows the number of rows represented by the bin. The next column shows the number of unique values in the bin. The last column shows the high value represented by the bin. In the example, bin 1 represents values from 1 to 75. Bin 2 represents values from 76 to 151.

Adjusting the Accuracy of the Statistics

You can increase the chance of accounting for all skewed data by simply increasing the number of "bins" in the distribution. By increasing the number of bins, you are decreasing the number of rows that are described in one set of statistics. You are also changing the definition of "highly duplicate" (remember that a highly duplicate value has >25% of the number of rows for one bin).

As an example, suppose you create a distribution on a column, such as **city**, for a table that holds 10,000 rows. You start out with 10 bins, which means that each bin holds approximately 10,000/10 = 1,000 rows. The distribution might be created as follows (only four bins are shown):

Atlanta- Chicago	Columbus- Dresden	Dublin- Hong Kong	Houston- Los Angeles	. . .
Bin 1: Unique: 20	Bin 2: Unique: 15	Bin 3: Unique: 3	Bin 4: Unique: 10	

In bin 1, there are 20 unique values represented. The optimizer will assume they are equally distributed, and project that there are 1,000/20 = 50 duplicate rows for each value between "Atlanta" and "Chicago."

Now let's say you increase the number of bins to 100 and re-create the distribution. Now each bin represents 10,000/100 = 100 rows! The distribution might look something like this:

Atlanta- Bangkok	Columbus- Chicago	Cincinnati- Dresden	Dublin- Hong Kong	. . .
Bin 1: Unique: 5	Bin 2: Unique: 15	Bin 3: Unique: 3	Bin 4: Unique: 10	

In bin 1, there are now five unique values represented. The optimizer will now project that there are 100/5 = 20 duplicates for every value between "Atlanta" and "Bangkok."

You can adjust the number of bins in the UPDATE STATISTICS statement using the RESOLUTION clause. A RESOLUTION of 1 means that 1% of the data will be represented by a bin, and there will be 100 bins. For example:

```
UPDATE STATISTICS MEDIUM ON table RESOLUTION 1
```

Finally, if you choose to create a distribution using a sample (MEDIUM), you can control how big a sample is used, with the combination of RESOLUTION and another value called CONFIDENCE. CONFIDENCE is a statistical measure of the reliability of the sample. As CONFIDENCE increases (up to .99) and the RESOLUTION value decreases (the number of bins increase), the sample size increases. To alter the CONFIDENCE from its default value of .95, include the clause in the UPDATE STATISTICS statement, for example:

```
UPDATE STATISTICS MEDIUM ON table RESOLUTION .1 CONFI-
DENCE .99
```

Generally, you do not have to adjust the CONFIDENCE from its default value.

So What Do I Do with These Distributions?

If you are happy with your query performance (who is?), don't bother with distributions. They involve some overhead to gather and create the distribution—reading and sorting the rows, creating the distribution, and storing it.

However, if your goal is ever-increasing performance and you can afford the overhead of creating distributions, you should run UPDATE STATISTICS MEDIUM on all columns that might possibly be used as a filter in a query. You can run UPDATE STATISTICS HIGH for columns with an index, because the presence of an index means that the column values won't have to be sorted for the distribution.

If, after creating distributions with this strategy, a query is still running poorly, follow these steps:

1.   Run and time the query using production data.

2.   Run the query with SET EXPLAIN ON to get the query path.

3.   Run UPDATE STATISTICS HIGH on all columns involved as filters in the query.

4.   Rerun and time the query.

5.   Run the query with SET EXPLAIN ON.

6.   If the query path is the same for step 2 and step 5, UPDATE STATISTICS HIGH will not affect the query. If the query path did change and the query time in step 4 is better than in step 1, UPDATE STATISTICS HIGH on the filter columns will positively affect performance!

7.9   IF ALL ELSE FAILS...

Sometimes, despite your efforts to index the appropriate columns and run UPDATE STA-
TISTICS properly, you deduce from the SET EXPLAIN output that the optimizer is still
choosing an incorrect path for a particular query, which adversely affects performance.
Many an administrator has dreamed of having an optimizer override features for these particular queries.

If all of the previous advice has not achieved what you think the optimal query path
should be, sometimes a few "tricks" can affect the optimizer's cost calculations enough to
get the results you want. Some of these tricks are:

1.   Index (or don't index) columns in small tables. As a rule, you usually want to index
     primary and foreign keys of all tables, regardless of the table size. The optimizer can
     then decide whether to use the index or read the table sequentially. However, by
     adding or dropping an index on these smaller tables, you can sometimes affect the
     query path positively.

2.   Run SET OPTIMIZATION LOW, even for queries with less than five tables. Some-
     times the change in paths that the optimizer examines may positively affect the final
     choice in query path.

3.   Alter the order of tables in the SELECT statement. Even though the order of tables
     in a query is not supposed to be significant, sometimes the order may matter if tables
     are similar in size and the optimizer costs are similar between two-way joins.

4.   Add extra, non-meaningful filters. Sometimes you can influence the optimizer by
     adding a filter in the WHERE clause. For example, a query can be rewritten from:

```
SELECT * from a,b,c where a.x = b.x and b.y = c.y
     where a.y = 20 and c.z = 30
```

to something like this:

```
SELECT * from a,b,c where a.x = b.x and b.y = c.y
     where a.y = 20 and c.z = 30 and c.y > 0
```

Extra filters give the optimizer incentive to choose the table earlier in the query path.
Remember that your goal in altering the query path is to put tables that can eliminate as
many rows as possible early in the path. In the example above, by adding a filter to table c
you might be able to influence the optimizer to put this table first in the path.

7.10   CASE STUDY 2 (VERSION 6.0 USING DISTRIBUTIONS)

The user complains of a slow response from a particular query, especially for the companies most often queried region, region 10000. You extract the actual SQL from the application, replace the variables with the values that the user was running with, and time the query:

```
time dbaccess db1 query.sql >outfile 2>outerr
```

The elapsed time is 10.8 seconds. Next, you execute SET EXPLAIN ON and rerun the query. The SET EXPLAIN output shows:

```
QUERY:
------
select * from account,store where account.region = 10000
    and store.location = 105
    and account.account_nbr = store.account_nbr

Estimated Cost: 77
Estimated # of Rows Returned: 1

1) informix.account: INDEX PATH

    (1) Index Keys: region
        Lower Index Filter: informix.account.region =
10000

2) informix.store: INDEX PATH

  Filters: informix.store.location = 105

  (1) Index Keys: account_nbr
        Lower Index Filter: informix.store.account_nbr =
informix.account.account_nbr
```

You first check that both tables are read with an index, evident by the INDEX PATH designation. You notice that the **account** table is chosen first in the path. Is this the optimal path? You run the following queries:

```
select count(*) from account where region = 10000
select count(*) from store where location = 105
```

The first SELECT returns 10,000 rows. The second SELECT returns 105 rows. Since the optimal path is usually one that eliminates as many rows as possible early in the query, it seems that in this case the **store** table should have been first in the query path. You wonder why the optimizer chose the path it did and check the statistics for the table, filter columns, and indexes for the filter columns.

```
select * from systables, syscolumns, sysindexes where
  syscolumns.colname = "region" and
  syscolumns.colno = sysindexes.part1 and
  sysindexes.tabid = systables.tabid and
  systables.tabname = "account"

select * from systables, syscolumns, sysindexes where
  syscolumns.colname = "location" and
  syscolumns.colno = sysindexes.part1 and
  sysindexes.tabid = systables.tabid and
  systables.tabname = "store"
```

You notice in the statistics listed by the SELECT statement that, for the **region** column, the **nunique** (number of unique values) statistic shows 1002. Since there are 11,000 rows in the **account** table, the number of duplicate rows projected per value is $11,000/1,002 = {\sim}11$. For the **location** column, the **nunique** statistic shows 111. Since there are 11,000 rows in the **store** table as well, the number of duplicates projected by the optimizer is $11,000/111 = {\sim}100$. The optimizer chose the correct path according to these statistics, assuming that approximately 11 rows would be chosen from the **account** table to join to the values in the **store** table.

The reality is that 1,000 rows were selected from the account table! This is a classic example of skewed data. The optimizer cannot discern skewed data without using data distributions. So you decide to create distributions for the **region, account_nbr**, and **location** columns. Since these columns all have indexes, you run UPDATE STATISTICS in HIGH mode.

```
    update statistics high for table account(region);
    update statistics high for table
account(account_nbr);
    update statistics high for table store(location);
    update statistics high for table
store(account_nbr);
```

Next, you rerun the query with SET EXPLAIN ON. The **sqexplain.out** file shows:

```
QUERY:
------
select * from account,store where region = 10000
    and location = 105
    and account.account_nbr = store.account_nbr


Estimated Cost: 170
Estimated # of Rows Returned: 9


1) informix.store: INDEX PATH


  (1)      Index Keys: location
           Lower Index Filter: informix.store.location =
105


2) informix.account: INDEX PATH


  Filters: informix.account.region = 10000


  (1)      Index Keys: account_nbr
           Lower Index Filter: informix.account.account_nbr
= informix.store.account_nbr
```

From this output, you see that the query path has changed, to SELECT first from the **store** table and join with the **account** table.

You then time the query again and find that, indeed, the change in query path has resulted in the query running several seconds faster. Although the gap in times between the two queries is small, it will become even more noticeable as both tables grow.

7.11   CHECKLIST FOR POORLY PERFORMING QUERIES

Table 7.1- Checklist for poorly performing queries

What to Check	How to Check	How to Alter
Has UPDATE STATISTICS been run?	Look for statistics entries in the **systables, syscolumns** and **sysindexes** tables.	UPDATE STATISTICS
Are filter columns in the SELECT statement indexed?	dbschema -d *database*	CREATE INDEX
Try SET OPTIMIZATION LOW for queries with > 4 tables		SET OPTIMIZATION LOW must be run before the query is optimized.
Create distributions on filter columns	dbschema -d *database* -hd	UPDATE STATISTICS MEDIUM or UPDATE STATISTICS HIGH

Chapter 8

Locking and Performance

The way locking is handled by applications can substantially affect the overall performance of an OnLine system. The potentially negative effect locking can have makes it an important area for the administrator to monitor. The administrator should audit application development processes to make sure that potentially damaging practices are avoided and the most efficient locking method is used.

The major topics discussed in this chapter are listed below.

• How locks work

• Lock levels

• Lock types

• Locking duration

• Locking recommendations

• Lock monitoring

8.1   HOW LOCKS WORK

Locks are used for *concurrency control*, or protecting one user's work from another. For example, when a row is updated, no other user should be able to change the row until the transaction that updates the row is committed. Even other readers should not be able to view the row until it is committed, because the change could be rolled back at any time during the transaction.

When a lock is placed on an item in a database, the item itself is not altered in any way. Instead, the locks are placed in a lock table, a structure in shared memory (see Figure 8.1).

Figure 8.1-   The lock table

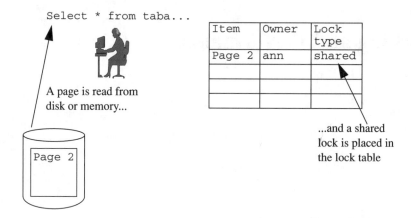

When another user must access or update an item, the user must first check the lock table to see if the lock exists there. If it does, the user will receive an error. Otherwise, if SET LOCK MODE TO WAIT is set in the application, the user will wait until the lock is released.

Locks are not only placed on data, but on indexes as well. When you update a row in a table that has two indexes, you will probably place at least three locks, one for the row and one for each index.

The administrator can specify, up to the system limit of 256,000, the number of locks that can be placed at any one time by all users (sessions) in the OnLine system. The configuration parameter that controls the size of the lock table is called LOCKS. If all users collectively require more locks than are specified by this parameter, the operations requesting the locks will fail. You can monitor if the LOCKS parameter is exceeded by running **onstat -p** (or, for 5.0, **tbstat -p**). In the sample **-p** output below (only a portion of the output is shown), the LOCKS value was exceeded five times.

```
ovtbls ovlock ovuserthread ovbuff usercpu  syscpu numckpts flushes

0      5      0            0      45.47   60.05  2        1042
```

The **ovlock** field in this output increments every time a user requests a lock and can't get one because the LOCKS parameter is exceeded.

8.2   LOCK LEVELS

There are three basic lock levels that can be applied in an OnLine system:

1. **Database locks**. Database locks prevent other users from adding or updating rows in any table or altering the structure of any table in the database. A database lock is placed by adding the EXCLUSIVE keyword to the DATABASE statement:

    ```
    DATABASE dbname EXCLUSIVE
    ```

2. **Table locks**. Table locks prevent other users from adding or updating rows in a specific table in the database. A table lock is placed by executing a LOCK TABLE statement in one of two forms. The first method shown below will allow other users to SELECT from rows in the table, but disallow any INSERT, UPDATE, or DELETE activity. The second method, with the IN EXCLUSIVE MODE clause shown below, disallows both update and most query activity (except for a specific execution of SELECT statement called *dirty reads* that do not check for locks).

    ```
    LOCK TABLE tabname
    LOCK TABLE tabname IN EXCLUSIVE MODE
    ```

3. **Page locks**. Page locks protect all rows or index items on a single data or index page.

4. **Row locks**. Row locks only protect specific rows or index keys.

    When a table is created, you specify whether the table will use row locks or page locks. If the DATABASE EXCLUSIVE or LOCK TABLE statements are not explicitly executed, the SQL statements run by a user will follow the locking mechanism (page or row) specified by the table.

    To create a table with row locking, use the LOCK MODE ROW clause, as shown below:

    ```
    CREATE TABLE tabname(col1 integer,...) LOCK MODE ROW;
    ```

    Page locking is the default method of locking. To create a table with page locking, omit the LOCK MODE clause or use the LOCK MODE PAGE option:

    ```
    CREATE TABLE tabname(col1 integer,...) LOCK MODE PAGE;
    ```

    Once the table is created, you can alter the lock level with the ALTER TABLE statement.

    ```
    ALTER TABLE tabname LOCK MODE (ROW)
    ```

    To determine if a table has row or page locking, look at the entry for the table in the system catalog table, **systables**.

    ```
    select locklevel from systables
       where tabname = "tabname";
    ```

A lock level of "P" means the table has page locking. A lock level of "R" means the table has row locking.

8.3 LOCK TYPES

Generally, there are four types of locks that can be put on a row or page. The type of lock held determines the amount of concurrency control on an item.

1. Shared locks. Shared locks allow other users to read an item but not to update it. Multiple shared locks can be placed on the same row. A user might want to place a shared lock on a row while it is being read to keep other users from changing the row's value.

2. Exclusive locks. Exclusive locks prevent other users from reading or updating the row. Exclusive locks are used when a row is INSERTed, UPDATEd, or DELETEd.

3. Update locks. Update locks are used when you fetch a row with an update cursor in an application. It is similar to a shared lock, except that it is *promotable* to an exclusive lock once the UPDATE actually occurs.

4. Intent locks. Intent locks are placed at the table or database level and prevent actions from occurring at the table level while users are executing operations at the row or page level. For example, if a user UPDATEs a row, you will see a lock placed at the row level as well as an intent lock placed at the table level.

Table 8.1 shows which locks are allowed on an item by another user if the first user already holds a lock on the same item. For example, if user 1 holds an exclusive lock on an item, no other lock is allowed by user 2 on the same item. However, if user 1 holds a shared lock on an item, user 2 can hold either a shared lock or an update lock on the item at the same time.

Table 8.1-Lock Interaction

User 2 requests

User 1 holds	Exclusive lock	Shared lock	Update lock
Exclusive lock	Not allowed	Not allowed	Not allowed
Shared lock	Not allowed	Allowed	Allowed
Update lock	Not allowed	Allowed	Not allowed

8.4   LOCK DURATION FOR **INSERT, UPDATE,** OR **DELETE**

When an UPDATE, INSERT, or DELETE statement places an exclusive lock on an item, how long it is held depends on the logging mode of the database and the type of transaction logic used in the application.

Databases without logging release locks immediately after the operation has completed.

Databases with logging use transaction logic to control lock duration. In many applications, SQL statements are part of a *transaction*; that is, statements that must be completed entirely or not at all. A transaction starts with a BEGIN WORK statement and completes with a COMMIT WORK statement for successful transactions, or a ROLLBACK WORK statement for unsuccessful transactions. A simple example of a transaction without the error-checking logic is shown below.

```
begin work;

insert into tab1 values (...); {Lock placed here}

update tab2 set x = x +1      {Lock(s) placed here}
    where x > 20;

commit work;                  {All locks released}
```

In this transaction, one row will be inserted into **tab1**, and one or more rows in **tab2** will be updated. The exclusive locks placed on each of the rows updated in **tab2** and the new row in **tab1** *remain until the end of the transaction*.

In some cases, a single SQL statement is not embedded between the BEGIN WORK or COMMIT WORK statement. In these cases, the SQL statement forms its own, or a *singleton,* transaction, and the COMMIT WORK is implied after the statement. In singleton transactions, the locks *remain until the end of the statement*.

8.5   LOCK DURATION FOR **SELECT** STATEMENTS—ISOLATION LEVELS

The lock duration for SELECT statements are determined by the type of *isolation level* used within an application. There are four isolation levels for SELECT statements:

1. **Dirty read.** The dirty read isolation level means that all locks are ignored by the SELECT statement, and no locks are placed on any rows that are read. If a database is not logged, all applications will read data with the dirty read isolation level. Dirty read is the most efficient isolation level. However, applications face the possibility

of reading rows that have been added or changed by another user but not committed. These uncommitted rows could possibly be "rolled back" (changed back to their previous values or deleted) after being read by an application using dirty read.

2. **Committed read**. The committed read isolation level means that each row fetched by a SELECT statement will be tested for the presence of a lock. If an exclusive lock is held by another user on the row or page, the FETCH or SELECT statement will receive an error. If SET LOCK MODE TO WAIT is set in the application, the application will wait until the lock has been released. Note that once the row is tested for locks, other users can then immediately place a lock on the row without the original reader knowing. This isolation level is the default for all logged databases.

3. **Cursor stability**. As the name implies, the cursor stability isolation level keeps the contents of the row stable the entire time the row is being examined in the application. It prevents the current row from being exclusively locked by another user by placing a shared lock on the item until the next row is fetched or the cursor is closed in the application.

4. **Repeatable read**. The repeatable read isolation level acquires a shared lock on every row examined by the SELECT statement. The shared locks are all held *until the end of the transaction*. This isolation level is often used by applications that cannot have new or updated rows in the set of information being read. For example, an application trying to obtain an account balance might need to make sure that new transactions are not being added while the account balance is being calculated. The repeatable read isolation level can potentially lock many rows, as even rows that are examined but not returned to the application are locked. This isolation level is the default isolation level of ANSI databases.

You change the isolation level from the default within an application by using the SET ISOLATION statement, for example:

```
SET ISOLATION TO CURSOR STABILITY
```

Applications accessing databases without logging cannot use the SET ISOLATION statement; only the dirty read isolation level will be used.

8.6 USING LOCKS EFFICIENTLY

How locks are used can affect the performance of the entire OnLine system. The database or system administrator should periodically monitor how the applications are using locks.

The goal in lock usage is to get the correct amount of concurrency control while:

• Minimizing the number of items locked. The more locks that are placed by one user, the higher the probability that other users must wait until these locks are released before continuing work.

• Minimizing how long the items are locked. The locks should only be held as long as necessary to obtain the correct amount of concurrency.

Here are some recommendations for using locks efficiently.

Avoid Using the Repeatable Read Isolation Level

The repeatable read isolation level potentially places locks on more items, and for a longer period of time, than the other isolation levels. Unless the application requires the use of repeatable read, avoid it. Remember that repeatable read is the default isolation level for databases created in ANSI mode.

Create Tables with Row-Level Locking

Row-level locking increases concurrency because the database server is locking the smallest-granularity item possible. Page locking means that even if only one row is being updated, all the rows on the page are unavailable. A table with a small row size can pack 50–100 rows on a single page. Index pages are even more dense; updating a key value for a table using page locking may lock 200 other key values!

Page-level locking should be used for tables that are usually updated with batch processes. When large numbers of rows are being UPDATEd or INSERTed at one time, only one page lock is placed for multiple rows. Using page locks may be the only way to avoid the 256,000 limit on the number of locks in the OnLine system.

Remember that page-level locking is the default locking level when a table is created, and you must specifically request row-level locking with the LOCK MODE ROW clause.

Use Dirty Read for Noncritical Applications

The dirty read isolation level means that no locks are placed or checked. An application will receive slightly better performance when dirty read is used. A common use for dirty read is in reports where reading uncommitted rows is acceptable. Also, nonvolatile tables are a good candidate for dirty read.

Keep Transactions Short to Avoid Concurrency Problems

Since locks are released at the end of the transaction, it makes sense to complete a transaction as quickly as possible. Keep interactive statements (statements that wait for input from a user) out of transaction logic if possible. Put only required logic between the BEGIN WORK and COMMIT WORK statements.

If possible, avoid transactions that update a large number of rows. Besides posing a concurrency problem, the transaction may become a *long transaction*. A long transaction is one that spans a certain percentage of logical logs—the percentage is specified by the LTXHWM configuration parameter. Long transactions will automatically be rolled back by the database server. Long transactions are a waste of resources, both the database server resources to roll back the transaction, and the lock resources that are not released until the transaction is rolled back.

If Possible, Lock the Table for Large Update Operations

The LOCK TABLE statement using the IN EXCLUSIVE MODE option places only one lock on the table, versus one lock for each row with row-level locking. By locking the table, you reduce the number of locks that are placed, resulting in slightly better performance. You also guard against the possibility that the transaction will fail because it reaches the maximum number of locks available in the OnLine system. Although LOCK TABLE reduces the availability of the table to other users, it enables a large update operation to be completed faster.

8.7   MONITORING LOCK USAGE

The administrator should suspect lock problems when specific applications are hung for short periods of time. By monitoring locks, you can see how many locks are held by each user as well as exactly what is being locked.

Monitoring Lock Usage with Version 5.0

The administrator can get a good idea of how often a user must wait for another user to release a lock with the **tbstat -p** command. The output of this command has a **lokwaits** column which is incremented every time a user waits for a lock.

```
bufwaits  lokwaits  lockreqs  deadlks dltouts  lchwaits  ckpwaits compress
13707        22      28175128  0         0      123442        1       65
```

In the output shown above, users had to wait for a lock to be released 22 times. You should monitor this value to see if it gets unusually high. If it does, you must monitor individual users and the number and type of locks they are holding.

To see exactly what locks are held, use the **tbstat -k** command. Here is a sample **tbstat -k** report:

```
Locks
address    wtlist    owner       lklist      type        tblsnum   rowid  size
10004ed8 0           10001cf8    0           HDR +X      1000002   207    0
10004f18 0           10001cf8    10004f78    HDR+IX      1000095   0      0
10004f58 0           10001cf8    10004f18    HDR+X       1000095   101    0
10004f78 0           10001cf8    10004ed8    HDR+S       1000002   208    0
10004f98 0           10001cf8    10004f58    HDR+X       1000095   102    0
  5 active, 1000 total, 64 hash buckets
```

There are several important fields in this report, and some are rather cryptic.

1. **address:** the internal address of the lock.

2. **wtlist:** the address of the first user that is waiting for the lock. You can find the actual process id of the user by looking for the address in **tbstat -u**.

3. **owner:** the address of the owner of the lock. To find the process id of the lock owner, look up the owner address in **tbstat -u**.

4. **type:** the type of lock held. The type of lock is specified by the characters after the "+". The possible lock types are:

    ```
    - X  = Exclusive lock
    - IX = Intent exclusive lock
    - IS = Intent shared lock
    - S  = Shared lock
    - U  = Update lock
    ```

5. **tblsnum:** the tblspace number (a unique identifier for the table). The first one or two digits are the dbspace number, as listed in **tbstat -d**, in which the table resides. The tblspace numbers ending in 02 are special database tablespaces used internally by the database server. To list the hexadecimal tblspace number for each table in a database, run the following SQL statement:

    ```
    select hex(partnum),tabname from systables
    ```
    Compare these values to the **tblsnum** column in **tbstat -d**.

6. **rowid:** identifies the actual item (row, table, or key) being locked. If the lock is on a table, the rowid is listed as 0. If the lock is on a page, the rowid ends in 00. For a key lock, the rowid will be listed as a large hexadecimal number. Otherwise, the value is a rowid and the lock is on a row.

7. **size:** is used for a special type of lock on varchar columns, called a byte lock.

The **-u** option of **tbstat** shows a few things about locks, including the number of locks held and whether the user is waiting for a lock. Here is an example of **tbstat -u** output:

```
Users

address  flags     pid  user      tty     wait tout locks  nreads nwrites

10001ba8 ------D  362  informix  ttyp1   0    0    0      126    3

10001c18 ------D  0    informix  ttyp1   0    0    0      0      0

10001c88 ------F  363  informix          0    0    0      0      0

10001cf8 --B----  387  george    ttyp1   0    0    5      6      11
```

If a user is waiting for a lock, the first column of the **flags** field would show an "l", and the **wait** column would show the actual address of the lock, which you can trace back to the lock list in **tbstat -l**.

In the example above, user **george** has five locks. You can see what locks **george** has by looking for the address 10001cf8 in the **owner** column of **tbstat -k**.

Monitoring Lock Usage with Version 6.0

The administrator can get a good idea of how often a user must wait for another user to release a lock with the **onstat -p** command. The output of this command has a **lokwaits** column which is incremented every time a user waits for a lock.

```
bufwaits   lokwaits   lockreqs  deadlks    dltouts ckpwaits compressseqscans

24708      40         8172128   0          0       2        80         161
```

In the output shown above, users had to wait for a lock to be released 40 times. You should monitor this value to see if it gets unusually high. If it does, you must monitor individual users and the number and type of locks they are holding.

Instead of using the **onstat** utility to monitor locks, consider using the SMI tables. SMI (System Monitoring Interface) is an SQL interface into the same memory structures that the **onstat** utility reads. To use SMI, select the **sysmaster** database from dbaccess. To list all users who own locks, run the following SQL statement:

```
select username,uid,waiter,dbsname,tabname,rowidlk,

    keynum,type

    from syslocks, syssessions

    where syssessions.sid = syslocks.owner
```

An example row from this output is shown below.

```
username    informix
uid         102
waiter
dbsname     bank1
tabname     transaction
rowidlk     0
keynum      0
type        X
```

The example shows a table lock on the **transaction** table. The rowidlk is listed as 0 if the lock is on a table. If any other session is waiting on the lock, the **session_id** is listed in the waiter column (however, only the first waiter is listed).

The lock type can be one of the following:

```
- X = Exclusive lock
- IX = Intent exclusive lock
- IS = Intent shared lock
- S = Shared lock
- U = Update lock
- SR = Shared repeatable read lock
```

You can also display the current locks in the system with **onstat -k**. A sample output is shown below. The description for the columns in **syslocks** closely mirror the fields in the **onstat -k** output.

```
Locks
address wtlist owner lklist type     tblsnum   rowid key#/bsiz
80f600  0      80a9d0 0      HDR+S    100002    205   0
80f628  0      80a9d0 80f600 HDR+X    100078    0     0
 2 active, 2000 total, 128 hash buckets
```

The fields in the lock output are explained below:

1. **address:** the internal address of the lock.

2. **wtlist:** the address of the first session that is waiting for the lock. You can find the actual session id of the user by looking for the address in **onstat -u**.

3. **owner:** the address of the owner of the lock. To find the session id of the owner, look up the address in **onstat -u**.

4.   **type:** the type of lock held. The type of lock is specified by the characters after the "+". The possible lock types are:

- X = Exclusive lock
- IX = Intent exclusive lock
- IS = Intent shared lock
- S = Shared lock
- U = Update lock
- SR = Shared repeatable read lock

5.   **tblsnum:** the tblspace number (a unique identifier for the table). The first one or two digits are the dbspace number, as listed in **onstat -d**, in which the table resides. The tblspace numbers ending in 02 are special database tablespaces used internally by the database server. To list the hexadecimal tblspace number for each table in a database, run the following SQL statement.

```
select hex(partnum),tabname from systables
```

Compare these values to the tblsnum column in **onstat -d**.

6.   **rowid:** the actual row being locked. If the lock is on a table, the rowid is 0. If the lock is on a page, the rowid ends in 00. If the value is a key lock, the rowid is the rowid of the row itself.

7.   **key#:** indicates that the lock is on a key. The key number starts with "k-".

8.   **size:** used for a special type of lock on varchar columns, called a byte lock.

The **-u** option of **onstat** shows a few things about locks, including the number of locks held and whether the user is waiting for a lock. Here is an example of **onstat -u** output:

```
Userthreads
address flags  sessid   user    tty  wait    tout locks nreads nwrites
806cc8  ---P--D 0        informix -    0        0    0     22     3
80702c  ---P--F 0        informix -    0        0    0     0      0
807390  ---P--B 8        informix -    0        0    0     0      0
8076f4  ---P--D 0        informix -    0        0    0     0      0
80a9d0  Y--P--- 16       joe      ttyp0 adb044  0    2     0      0
80ad34  L--PR-- 18       ann      ttyp0 80f628  -1   1     0      0
  6 active, 20 total
```

If a user is waiting for a lock, the first column of the **flags** field shows an "L", and the **wait** column would show the actual address of the lock, which you can trace back to the lock list in **onstat -k**.

In the example above, user **joe** has one lock. You can see which lock **joe** has by looking for the address 80a9d0 in the **owner** column of **onstat -k**, shown earlier in this section. Also, the output shows **ann** waiting for a lock. From looking up the address of the lock for which **ann** is waiting in the onstat -u output (80f628), you can determine that **joe** owns the lock.

8.8   CASE STUDY (USING VERSION 5.0)

This case study uses sample output for version 5.0. However, the output would be very similar if version 6.0 was used.

Several users call you, the administrator, complaining that their "applications are hung." After ruling out the usual causes, such as full logs and a problem with the OnLine system (you can log in and access data with dbaccess), you decide to take a look at individual user activity with **tbstat -u**.

```
Users
address    flags    pid  user     tty     wait       tout   locks   nreads  nwrites
10001ba8 ------D 362    informix ttyp1 0          0      0       126     3
10001c18 ------D 0      informix ttyp1 0          0      0       0       0
10001c88 ------F 363    informix       0          0      0       0       0
10001cf8 --B---- 387    sandy    ttyp1 0          0      10384   21009   30438
10001d68 L---R-- 407    vijay    ttyp0 10004f58 -1      1       0       0
10001dd8 L---R-- 414    victor   ttyp3 10004f58 -1      1       0       0
```

You locate the users who have complained (**vijay** and **victor**) and notice from the flags field that they are both waiting for a lock. To find out who is holding the lock, you note the lock address in the wait column (10004f58) and find the entry with the same lock address in **tbstat -k**.

```
Locks
address    wtlist   owner    lklist     type     tblsnum rowid size
10004ed8 0          10001cf8 0          HDR+X    1000002 207 0
10004ef8 0          10001dd8 0          S        1000002 208 0
10004f18 0          10001cf8 10004f78HDR+IX 1000095 0   0
10004f38 0          10001d68 0          S        1000002 208 0
10004f58 10001d68 10001cf8 10004f18HDR+X 1000095 100 0
10004f78 0          10001cf8 10004ed8 HDR+S   1000002 208 0
```

Lock 10004f58 belongs to user 10001cf8. You look back in the first column of **tbstat -u** and find that user 10001cf8 is **sandy**. **Sandy** is in transaction (as indicated by the "B" in the second position of the flags column) and is currently holding 10,384 locks. This seems excessive, so you give Sandy a call and find out that she is running a batch update process. You make a note to talk to the systems analyst to see if the transaction can be run at night or broken up into smaller transactions.

You also notice something interesting about the lock for which Vijay and Victor are waiting. The rowid for the lock is 100. Since the rowid ends in 0, you know that the lock is on a page, not a specific row. This can seriously degrade concurrency and might be the reason several users are waiting. To find the table that has page-level locking, you look at the **tblsnum** column for the tablespace number, which is 1000095. You convert the number to decimal (16777365) and look up the table name in the **partnum** column of **systables**.

```
    select tabname from systables where partnum =
16777365
```

You make a note to change the table to row-level locking tonight after the production users go home.

8.9   CHECKLIST FOR MONITORING LOCKS

Table 8.2-Checklist for monitoring locks

What to Check	How to Check	How to Alter
Lock waits	onstat -p or tbstat -p (lockwaits column)	Change locking strategy in applications
Is the lock table large enough?	ovlock field in tbstat -p (onstat -p)	LOCKS configuration parameter
Are applications using repeatable read?	Look for SET ISOLATION statements. ANSI databases use repeatable read as default	SET ISOLATION TO COMMITTED READ or SET ISOLATION TO CURSOR STABILITY
Do tables use row-level locking	`select locklevel from systables` where tabname = "*tabname*"	ALTER TABLE
Is dirty read used for reports or large queries using non-volatile tables?	Look for SET ISOLATION statements.	SET ISOLATION TO DIRTY READ

Table 8.2-Checklist for monitoring locks (Continued)

What to Check	How to Check	How to Alter
Can large update operations lock the table?		LOCK TABLE tabname IN EXCLUSIVE MODE
Are transactions as compact as possible?	Look for extraneous statements within transaction logic	Eliminate all unneeded code within a transaction

Chapter 9

Other Ways to Improve Performance

There are certain activities that may require a special configuration of the OnLine system. This chapter outlines the steps you can take to make these activities perform better.

The activities discussed in this chapter are:

- Data loads
- Indexing
- Batch delete programs
- Archiving
- High connection and network traffic load

9.1 DATA LOADS

Many applications require that a large amount of data be loaded into a table or set of tables, usually from an external source, such as a telephone switch or a mainframe database. Sometimes a load may occur only once when data is converted from a different file format into an Informix database. Often the load program is run at off-peak hours, and possibly has exclusive use of the tables. Some suggestions for improving performance in this kind of activity are listed below.

Increase the Checkpoint Interval

Checkpoints take precious time away from inserting data into a database. Since the data load will usually be INSERTing data into a small number of pages (unless the table has more than one index), the disk writes should be concentrated on a small number of pages.

If checkpoints normally occur every 10 minutes or less, consider increasing the checkpoint to 15 or 20 minutes for the data load. Unfortunately, to do this, you will have to increase CKPTINTVL and restart the OnLine system. Also, the physical log must be big enough to handle the before image of pages written during the checkpoint interval.

Drop Indexes

A data load will proceed much faster without indexes on the table being loaded. If the data load is running when other users are not using the system, and the number of rows being loaded is greater than approximately one-third of the number of rows in the table, dropping the indexes is advantageous. If the OnLine system is version 6.0, performance will improve dramatically with this method, because index builds are much faster in this version of the OnLine product.

Also, if the table contains any constraints, these should be dropped with the ALTER TABLE statement before the load proceeds. Constraints are usually enforced by an index.

Use INSERT Cursors

INSERT cursors are usually the fastest method of putting data in a table. INSERT cursors buffer rows in the front end before sending them to the database server to process. You can get significantly better performance by using INSERT cursors to load data rather than an INSERT statement because of the decrease in the amount of messages that must be passed between the application and database server.

The only difficulty of using INSERT cursors is that if a failure occurs for some reason, it is difficult to determine which row caused the failure. The added error checking requires some extra coding in the application.

PREPARE Statements that Are Used Repeatedly

If you are unable to use an INSERT cursor because of error-checking difficulties, the INSERT statement should be PREPAREd first and EXECUTEd repeatedly. The PREPARE statement parses the SQL statement once, and cuts down on the amount of message passing and the work done by the database server when the statement is executed many times.

Use LOAD Instead of the dbload Utility

The LOAD command is more efficient than the **dbload** utility for loading formatted data from a sequential file. Unfortunately, the LOAD command is very simple and lacks some of the features available with dbload. For the best performance use LOAD; or, if you need a more controlled environment, use INSERT cursors.

9.2   INDEXING

Index creation (see Figure 9.1) is an operation all administrators wish ran faster, because the table is locked and unavailable during the index build. Version 6.0 has added a parallel index build feature which allows indexes to be built even faster than in version 5.0.

An index build consists of the following activities:

1.   The data is read from disk into the buffer pool, unless it is already cached in the buffer pool.

2.   The key is extracted and sorted. The preliminary sort dramatically improves the performance of the index build because the b-tree pages can be filled sequentially. The sort uses memory for smaller tables. For larger tables, both memory and disk are used to sort the keys.

3.   The b-tree is built with the sorted keys. In version 6.0, larger indexes will be built in parallel, with each thread building a part of the subtree which is finally put together into one b-tree.

Figure 9.1-   How an index is created

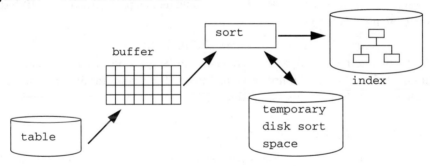

There are a few things you can do to improve performance of index builds.

Perform Parallel Sorts

The sort routine itself takes up a good percentage of the time needed to create the index. To speed up the sort, you can use the parallel sort routine. Parallel sorting is activated by setting the PSORT_NPROCS environment variable to the number of processes (or threads in version 6.0) that will perform the sort. The environment variable should be set before starting the application process that runs the CREATE INDEX statement.

Although parallel sorting shows the most performance gain with a multi-processor system, a single-processor system may benefit from PSORT_NPROCS set to 2. Even though there is only one processor to perform the work, one sort routine may be waiting for a disk read or write, while the other may be using the processor.

Spread Sort Files Across Disks

Sorting large tables will usually mean that the sort routine cannot do all its work in memory, and temporary sort runs must be written to disk. To decrease disk contention, spread the temporary sort files across disks.

In version 5.0, temporary sort files are written to one or more file system directories. If you are running a parallel sort, you can set the environment variable PSORT_DBTEMP to multiple directories.

```
PSORT_NPROCS = /sortdir1:/sortdir2
```

The first sort file will be created in **/sortdir1**, the second in **/sortdir2**, the third in **/sortdir1**, and so on. Obviously, these two directories should be in file systems on different disks.

In version 6.0, you can send temporary sort files to dbspaces, preferable to using UNIX directories because the chunks are usually a raw device. To set the location of multiple sort files, use either the DBSPACETEMP configuration parameter or the DBSPACE-TEMP environment variable.

```
DBSPACETEMP = dbtemp1,dbtemp2
```

The first sort file will be created in the **dbtemp1** dbspace, the second in the **dbtemp2** dbspace, the third in **dbtemp1**, and so on. The chunks for **dbtemp1** should be on a different disk than the chunks for **dbtemp2**.

Increase Read-Ahead Parameters (6.0)

In version 6.0, the read-ahead parameters allow the I/O subsystem (either the AIO vps or kernel AIO) to attempt to read pages from disk into the shared memory buffer pool before they are needed by the session. Since an index build must read every page in the table, it is an excellent candidate to take advantage of read-ahead. You may consider increasing RA_PAGES to make sure that enough pages are read into shared memory to keep up with the index build process.

9.3   LARGE DELETE OPERATIONS

Another operation that causes great upheaval in an OnLine system is one that removes a large number of rows from one or more tables. Sometimes a DELETE operation is combined with an operation that moves these rows to an archive or history table.

Here are some recommendations for improving performance for a large DELETE operation.

Drop Indexes First

When a row is deleted, the database server must find the key in each index and delete it as well as the actual row itself. In large indexes with three or four levels, this might mean a few extra disk reads for each index. Depending on the number of rows you are deleting, it may be faster to drop indexes first, before deleting a large number of rows.

Another reason to drop indexes first is that a massive delete operation may leave the existing index very sparsely populated, hurting performance on subsequent operations that use the index. You can see the average number of free bytes per index node of an index by running the following command:

```
oncheck -pT database:table
```

If the b-tree pages are less than half full on average, you will substantially decrease the size of the index by rebuilding.

Since the table is locked while the index is being created, dropping indexes before a DELETE operation may not be feasible for databases used 24 hours a day.

Lock the Table in Exclusive Mode

If the delete operation is using the table exclusively, lock the table before deleting rows.

```
LOCK TABLE tabname IN EXCLUSIVE MODE
```

Locking the table decreases the amount of locking operations that must occur for each DELETE statement. It also decreases the chance that you will run out of OnLine locks during the delete operation. Finally, for version 6.0, locking the table decreases the overhead of marking the row for DELETE and directing the btree-cleaner thread to DELETE the row when the transaction is committed.

Avoid a Long Transaction

A long transaction is a transaction that starts in the first log and spans a percentage of the logs given by the LTXHWM configuration parameter. A long transaction will be rolled back by the database server.

If your application deletes a large number of rows in one transaction, you should make sure there is enough log space to hold the transaction. One entry is placed in the logical log for every row deleted and for every index key deleted. To make a rough estimation of the amount of space used by a DELETE transaction, run a DELETE statement that only deletes a small number of rows. Then you can examine the logs to see how much log space was used with **tbstat -l** or **onstat -l**, or run the **tblog** utility to see the size of each log entry:

1. Run the following command (note that the resulting file may be very large) to dump the log files on disk:

        tblog >tblog.out

2. Examine the tblog.out file with an editor. Look for DELITEM (index key delete) and HDELETE (row delete) transaction types. The **len** field will give you an idea of how long each transaction record is. A sample entry is shown below.

        addr   len   type   xid   id   link

        18   40   DELITEM 5   1   1f37c4 100039 3915 199 3 4

Guarding against long transactions is not exactly providing a performance improvement. However, the consequences of a long transaction do impact performance. If a long transaction occurs, it is rolled back, which takes almost as much time as performing the transaction itself.

9.4 IMPROVING ARCHIVE PERFORMANCE

An archive is a necessary part of the daily activity of a system, but it negatively impacts the performance of other processing that is occurring at the same time, especially for an OnLine system running 24 hours a day. Normally, an archive should be planned for the time of day when there is the least amount of activity in the OnLine system.

Here are some suggestions for improving the performance of an archive.

Invest in a Fast Tape Drive

In version 5.0, this is the best advice for improving overall performance, since multiple tape drives cannot be used.

OnLine allows archives to remote tape devices. However, the extra network operations required to transfer data across the network will impact archive performance.

Use Parallel Archiving (Version 6.0)

The ON-Archive utility in version 6.0 allows for parallel archiving of dbspaces (see Figure 9.2). This means that if you have multiple tape drives, they can be used to archive the OnLine system in parallel. One or more dbspaces can be assigned to a particular dbspace set, which then can be archived to a specific tape drive.

Figure 9.2- Parallel archiving

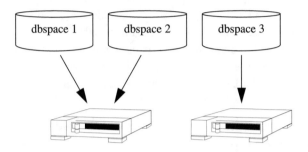

Parallel archiving will be most efficient when the tables can be spread evenly between the tape drives. Keep this in mind when planning locations of tables and dbspaces.

Archive Only Active Tables Nightly (Version 6.0)

The ON-Archive utility in version 6.0 allows you to archive only specific dbspaces. This feature gives you extensive freedom in planning nightly backups. Consider archiving the most used tables nightly and static tables less often. However, a restore may take longer with this method, because the restore must cycle through all the log tapes looking for transactions for that table, even though there may be none.

Move Very Large Tables to Another OnLine System (Version 5.0)

In version 5.0, you do not have very many options for archiving very large data-bases, because the entire OnLine system must be archived at once. Also, it is important to consider the time to complete a restore process on a large database.

One way to cut down on archive and restore time is to move very large tables to another OnLine system. The OnLine system can be on the same machine as the first OnLine system or a remote machine. Since each OnLine system has its own archive and restore processes, you can restore or archive both OnLine systems in parallel. This strat-egy works best with tables that are not used often, such as history tables, because of the added overhead of accessing a table in another OnLine system.

9.5   CONFIGURING THE ONLINE SYSTEM FOR A LARGE NUMBER OF CONNECTIONS

An OnLine system with a large number of user connections will have its own performance bottlenecks which the administrator should plan to avoid. Usually, when there is a large number of connections the application processes will reside on one or more client systems, different from the system the database server resides on. This configuration is most common because most UNIX systems simply cannot handle a database server and a large number of application processes simultaneously.

Here are some suggestions on how to achieve the best performance in a heavily used client/server environment.

Guard Against Network Overload

One or more network packets will be sent to the database server every time the application processes an SQL statement. The database server sends one or more network packets when data must be returned to the application or an SQL statement has completed execution. And of course, when an application connects to the database server, a message must be sent to initiate the connection request.

All of these messages can add up to a network overload when hundreds or even thousands of users are connected. If a network is overloaded, the number of packet collisions (where multiple users try to send a packet over the network at one time) increase. You can see the number of packet collisions in your system by running the UNIX **netstat** utility. The following example shows the network packets and collisions every two seconds, with the first line showing statistics since the system was last rebooted.

```
netstat -i 2
  input (lo0) output            input    (Total)    output
 packets errs packets errs colls packets errs packets errs colls
  83391   0    83391   0    200   83391  0    83395  2    23
  229     0    229     0    0     229    0    229    0    0
  68      0    68      0    0     68     0    68     0    0
  66      0    66      0    0     66     0    66     0    0
```

This example shows very few collisions for the number of packets that have been sent and received.

If your network is overloaded, consider breaking the network into sub-networks. With version 6.0 of OnLine, you can divide connections up into multiple network interface cards. To do this, you need two entries in the /etc/hosts file, two entries in the **$INFORMIXDIR/etc/sqlhosts** file, and two entries in the /etc/services file.

The **$INFORMIXDIR/etc/sqlhosts** file might look something like this:

```
interface1   onsoctcp   hostname1 soc1
interface2   onsoctcp   hostname2 soc2
```

The /etc/hosts file will have two entries, one for each network interface card.

```
192.133.104.19   hostname1
192.133.104.20   hostname2
```

The application will connect using one of the interface cards; you specify which with the INFORMIXSERVER environment variable. This example shows how to set the environment variable using the Bourne shell:

```
INFORMIXSERVER=interface1
export INFORMIXSERVER
```

Finally, you must have both server names, **interface1** and **interface2**, in the OnLine configuration file.

```
DBSERVERNAME interface1
DBSERVERALIAS interface2
```

Decrease the Message Traffic if the Network Is Slow

If network traffic is a problem, or the client and server are separated by a slow wide-area network, make sure the number of network messages is kept to a minimum.

- PREPARE statements that are reused whenever possible. The PREPARE statement performs the initial parse of the SQL statement. Once a statement is prepared, the subsequent execution does not have to perform the parse operation again, cutting down on the number of messages passed back and forth between the application and the database server.

- Use stored procedures for activities that execute more than three SQL statements without passing messages back to the application. Although stored procedures have their own overhead, they are most efficient when there are multiple SQL statements that must be executed together. If these statements do not pass messages back to the user, they are even more efficient when executed in a stored procedure.

- Don't return rows or columns unless they are needed by the application. Sometimes novice programmers retrieve more data with an SQL statement than is needed and eliminate unneeded data in the application. This is a poor programming practice, especially when the network can be a bottleneck.

Increase the Number of Poll Threads (6.0)

OnLine version 6.0 receives messages from the client application through a specific thread called the poll thread. If many applications are trying to send messages at the same time, the poll thread may not be able to keep up. For more than 50 active users connecting through TCP/IP, you may benefit through an increase in the number of poll threads. Shared memory connections use a poll thread as well, but the shared memory poll thread has much less work to do than the TCP/IP poll thread and can handle more users.

The NETTYPE configuration parameter specifies, among other things, the number of poll threads that will be started. The number of poll threads is specified in the second field in the NETTYPE parameter. The example below shows two poll threads configured for the TCP/IP TLI protocol.

```
NETTYPE TLITCP,2,100,CPU
```

Another important field in NETTYPE specifies the vp on which the poll thread(s) run. The fourth field can either specify CPU, for the CPU vp, or NET, for the network vp. You should place the poll threads for the most important protocol used in your system on the CPU vp. Only one poll thread can run on a single vp. If users communicate through either shared memory or TCP/IP, the poll thread from one protocol should run on the CPU vp, while the poll thread for the other protocol runs on the network vp; for example:

```
NETTYPE TLITCP,2,100,CPU

NETTYPE IPCSHM,1,50,NET
```

Since only one poll thread can run on a vp, the above configuration requires that two CPU vps be running; otherwise, only one poll thread will be started. Set the number of CPU vps with the NUMCPUVPS configuration parameter.

Increase the Number of Listen Threads (6.0)

Although the poll thread handles all incoming messages, any message that is a new connection is passed off for processing to another thread, called the *listen* thread.

If a large number of sessions (over 200–300) will be connecting at one time, the listen thread must handle all these connections. You may get better initial connection performance by adding more than one listen thread in addition to having more than one poll thread.

To start two listen threads, use two TCP/IP ports (usually defined in **/etc/services**) and specify two dbservernames in the ONCONFIG file. In addition, you will need two entries in the sqlhosts file.

The **sqlhosts** file will look something like this:

```
dbservername1    ontlitcp   hostname     port1
dbservername2    ontlitcp   hostname     port1
```

The entries in the ONCONFIG file are:

```
DBSERVERNAME dbservername1
DBSERVERALIASES dbservername2
```

Before connecting, the user must set INFORMIXSERVER to either dbservername1 or dbservername2.

To check if multiple listen threads were started, run **onstat -g ath** to list all threads. Look for thread names that contain the "listen" keyword.

Chapter 10

Fragmentation and Parallel Database Query

Version 7.0 of INFORMIX-OnLine Dynamic Server has two features very important to performance: *Parallel Database Query* (PDQ) and *Fragmentation*. Both features promise to improve performance in some OnLine activities, most notably in decision support queries. This chapter will discuss the two features and how they can be utilized to improve performance. Some of the topics covered are:

- What is fragmentation?
- Strategies for fragmentation
- What is Parallel Database Query?
- How to monitor and tune PDQ

10.1 WHAT IS FRAGMENTATION?

Fragmentation is a method of intelligently spreading a table across disks to improve performance. Although earlier versions of OnLine had a method of striping a table across disks by adding multiple chunks from different disks to the same dbspace, you could not easily control how the data was sent to each chunk.

Some of the advantages of fragmentation are:

- Fragmentation is a key component of Parallel Data Query, allowing OnLine to scan each fragment in parallel to read large amounts of data quickly.
- Some queries or other SQL operations may need to search only one fragment on one disk, rather than through the entire table.
- If many users are executing operations on a fragmented table concurrently, a table spread across many disks may cut down on disk contention between users.

How a Table Is Fragmented

Each fragment resides on a different dbspace. To fragment a table across disks, chunks for each dbspace should reside on different disks. When you create or decide to fragment a table, you specify which part of the table will reside on each dbspace (see Figure 10.1).

Figure 10.1- A fragmented table

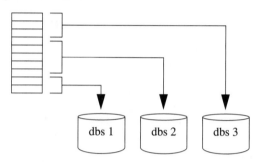

There are two methods of fragmenting a table:

• Round robin. This method randomly places rows on one of the fragments for a table. An example of a table created with round-robin fragmentation on two fragments is shown below.

```
create table customer(
    customer_num    serial
    customer_lname  char(20))
    fragment by round robin in dbs1,dbs2;
```

• Expression-based. This method places rows on a fragment based on an expression. For example, you may want to place all rows where **employee_lname** are between A and L in one fragment, and all rows where **employee_lname** are between M and Z in another fragment. An example of a table created with expression-based fragmentation is shown below.

```
create table customer(
    customer_num  serial
    customer_lname char(20))
    fragment by expression
        customer_lname >= "A" and
        customer_lname <= "L" in dbs1,
          customer_lname > "L" in dbs2;
```

Each fragment is put in its own set of extents with its own tablespace number.

You can also fragment an index. By default, an index of a fragmented table is fragmented in the same way as the table. You can also create an index with its own fragmentation scheme.

```
create index idx1 on customer(customer_num)
     fragment by expression
     customer_num < 100000 in dbs1,
     customer_num >= 100000 in dbs2;
```

When an index is fragmented, each fragment is put in its own set of extents with its own tablespace number. This means that the index pages are not intermingled with data pages, as they are in unfragmented tables.

The disk layout for the example fragmentation of the customer table is shown in Figure 10.2.

Figure 10.2- Sample fragmentation diagram

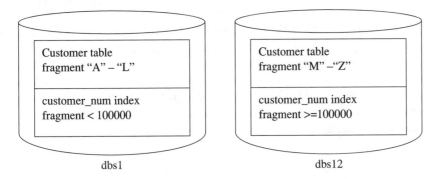

An index can be moved to a different dbspace than the data without being fragmented.

```
create index idx1 on customer(customer_num)
          in dbs2;
```

How OnLine Uses a Fragmented Table and Index

Suppose the **customer** table is fragmented by **customer_lname,** and its index is fragmented by **customer_num,** as shown in the previous example. A decision support query executed on this table might be:

```
select * from customer group by customer_num
```

In this example, all fragments must be scanned, since **customer_lname** is not included as a filter in the query. For a decision support query (a query that will read a large amount of data), one thread will be assigned to scan each fragment.

Consider the following query:

```
select * from customer where customer_lname > "N"
```

In this example, the optimizer can determine from the fragmentation expression that only the second fragment must be read, so only one thread will be started to scan that fragment. The other fragments will not be read.

What happens if a decision support query can use an index, such as the following query?

```
select * from customer where customer_num > 120000
```

In this case, since the **customer_num** index is fragmented by **customer_num**, only one index fragment will be read to find the location of the data. The best scenario would be if the index fragment read is significantly smaller than the entire index would be if it was not fragmented.

10.2   STRATEGIES FOR FRAGMENTATION

The suggestions below are for achieving the best performance by fragmenting a table and its indexes.

- Fragment to spread I/O across disks. The decision support query will start a scan thread for each fragment it must read. The scan threads should have an equal amount of work to do.

- Don't over-fragment. Each fragment for a table should reside on a separate disk. There is some overhead to opening a fragment to scan, so don't create very small fragments. Also, don't bother fragmenting tables and indexes that aren't used often.

- Keep fragmentation expressions simple. Overly complicated expressions might confuse the optimizer, which must determine what fragments should be read for a query. The SET EXPLAIN output shows which fragments will be read. You should plan to test your fragmentation scheme against production queries using a test database first. The following is a sample output of SET EXPLAIN which shows that all fragments will be scanned for the query.

```
QUERY:

------

select number from account order by number
```

```
Estimated Cost: 2
Estimated # of Rows Returned: 10
Temporary Files Required For: Order By

1)informix.account: SEQUENTIAL SCAN(Parallel,
                                fragments: ALL)
```

- Generally, fragment indexes by their key values. Queries that can use only one or two index fragments will benefit by the smaller number of index pages. Fragmenting indexes increases concurrency because different users may be reading different fragments at one time.
- Don't fragment tables on columns whose values change frequently. If the column is updated, the row or key value might need to be moved from one fragment to another, resulting in some processing overhead. Also, fragmentation on date columns or any other rapidly increasing column may cause the administrator to constantly rearrange the fragmentation scheme.
- Choose round-robin fragmentation only when the table is usually read sequentially (usually in queries without a WHERE clause) or when there is no column that can be used to evenly spread data across disks.
- Don't index columns unless they are used for OLTP queries. In earlier versions of OnLine, a query executed very slowly if it could not use an index. With the advent of hash joins (a new method of joining tables) and parallel scans, it might be much faster for the database server to scan the data sequentially rather than use the index. Although the optimizer should make this determination, sometimes it will not be able to give the information it has.

Note that there are other considerations in fragmenting tables and indexes, such as archiving, fault tolerance, and administration. These issues are not covered in this book but should be analyzed by the administrator before embarking on a fragmentation strategy.

10.3 CASE STUDY

To illustrate fragmentation guidelines, here is an example of how a table might be fragmented. The table is called **transaction**, and holds all transactions for an account.

```
create table transaction(
        trans_id      serial,
        trans_amt     money(12,2),
        trans_date    date,
        trans_type    char(2),
        account_nbr   integer)
```

```
create index idx1 on transaction(account_nbr);
create index idx2 on transaction(trans_date);
```

Before deciding on a fragmentation strategy, you first examine how the data is used. The most methodical way to do this is to examine key applications and extract the queries. You determine the most important queries and how often they are executed. You pinpoint one very important decision support query that is used to produce a nightly transaction report.

```
select * from account, transaction
    where account.account_nbr = transaction.account_nbr
        group by trans_type
```

You also examine and pinpoint the most important OLTP query; that is, a query that examines only a few rows. Usually, OLTP queries must be completed quickly. The crucial OLTP query you identify is:

```
select * from account, transaction
    where account.account_nbr = transaction.account_nbr
    and account_nbr = ?
```

Probably the best table fragmentation scheme would be one that would spread the decision support query across multiple disks. There may be a few columns that can be used to fragment data, but the administrator determines that the **trans_type** (transaction type) column might produce a good spread.

The best index fragmentation scheme for **idx1** is on **account_nbr**, since a query on the index need only read one fragment. Even though **account_nbr** is a serial field in another table (**account**), you determine that account numbers do not get assigned very quickly, and a fragmentation scheme on this value may be fairly stable.

It might not be a good idea to fragment the **idx2** index at all. The **trans_date** column is not a good candidate because date columns tend to constantly increase, causing the administrator to create new fragments for the newer dates and deleting fragments with older dates. Instead, you decide to put the index in a separate dbspace.

The schema for our newly fragmented table might look something like this:

```
create table transaction(
            trans_id        serial,
            trans_amt       money(12,2),
            trans_date      date,
            trans_type      char(2),
            account_nbr     integer)
```

```
fragment by expression
        trans_type = "d" or trans_type = "c" in dbs1,
        trans_type = "e" or trans_type = "m" in dbs2,
        remainder in dbs3;

create index idx1 on transaction(account_nbr)
        fragment by expression
            account_nbr < 100000 in dbs4,
            account_nbr >= 100000 and account_nbr < 200000
                            in dbs5,
            account_nbr >= 200000 in dbs6;

create index idx2 on transaction(trans_date) in dbs6;
```

10.4   PARALLEL DATABASE QUERY

Another very important feature to performance in an OnLine system is Parallel Database Query, or PDQ. PDQ is a method to parallelize a *decision support query*, or a query that must work with many rows in one or more tables. PDQ is effective on multiprocessor systems with multiple disks.

The database server divides a decision support query into multiple pieces and gives each piece to a separate thread. In most cases, the threads can do their work in parallel. For example, two scan threads that scan data from disk can work in parallel.

The threads started to perform the query, all run on the CPU virtual processor. Since all CPU vps share the same ready queue, this means that the threads may or may not be running at once. The true degree of parallelism also depends on the other activity in the OnLine system, since there are other operations running in an OnLine system and sharing the CPU vp.

The following diagram shows that the relationship between threads and virtual processors is variable. The diagram shows that two threads are running in parallel, one that scans data and one that joins the data from one table to another. There are several other threads involved in the query (another scan thread and a join thread) waiting for a CPU vp to become free so they can run. Other users' threads can also be in the ready queue or running on a CPU vp. The relationship between virtual processors and hardware processors in a system may also be variable, depending on the other work that is occurring in the system. In Figure 10.3, the two CPU vps are running on two separate processors. However, at any time, the processes may be replaced by other processes in the system needing to perform work.

Figure 10.3- Parallel Data Query—threads, vps, and processors

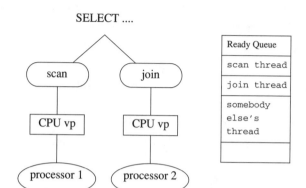

10.5 HOW TO MONITOR AND TUNE PDQ

Left unchecked, a decision support query could spawn 10 or 20 threads that would use all the available resources on the system. Imagine what multiple decision support queries could do to a system!

Although the fastest way to perform a query is to give the query all the resources it could possibly use, other work may need to be completed during the same time frame. The administrator has the ability to determine how much *resource*, meaning memory and CPU, can be used to perform a query. Once the administrator specifies the amount of resource a query can have, it is up to a part of the database server called the *Memory Grant Manager* to determine whether a query can proceed with the amount of resources it has requested.

The configuration parameters that control PDQ are listed below:

• PDQPRIORITY: The PDQPRIORITY configuration parameter sets the amount of resources that will be used by an individual query. If PDQPRIORITY is set to 0, no parallelism is used—the query runs as it would with earlier versions. If PDQPRIORITY is set to 1, scan threads are started in parallel (one per disk involved in the fragment), but no other parallelism is used in the query. If PDQPRIORITY is set from 2 to 100, some parallelism beyond multiple scan threads is used. In this case, you can think of PDQPRIORITY as a percentage of the total amount of resource the query uses in comparison to how much it would receive if it could get as much as it wanted. For example, if PDQPRIORITY is set to 50, a query would run with 50% of the number of threads and memory it would use at 100%. PDQPRIORITY can also be used as an environment variable for a particular application's session, or in a program (with the SET PDQPRIORITY statement) to override the configuration parameter.

- MAX_PDQPRIORITY: Since PDQPRIORITY can be set by an application developer or a user, MAX_PDQPRIORITY allows the administrator to make sure that users do not request 100% of available resource. The PDQPRIORITY is multiplied by (MAX_PDQPRIORITY/100) to obtain the actual priority that is used. For example, if PDQPRIORITY is set by a session at 100, and MAX_PDQPRIORITY is set to 50, then the true priority used for the query is 100 * (50/100) = 50.

- DS_TOTAL_MEMORY: The administrator can also cap the amount of shared memory used for decision support queries with the DS_TOTAL_MEMORY configuration parameter. DS_TOTAL_MEMORY is a subset of the shared memory that is allocated to the entire OnLine system. It is allocated from the virtual shared memory for the OnLine system.

- DS_MAX_QUERIES: The DS_MAX_QUERIES parameter specifies the number of decision support queries that can run at once. If DS_MAX_QUERIES is set to 5, only five queries that are classified as decision support queries can run at once. All other queries must wait until a running query completes. All non-decision support queries can run at any time.

The PDQ parameters can also be set dynamically with the **onmode utility**.

These parameters give the administrator a great deal of flexibility; however, they can be difficult to tune. For example, the administrator may need to decide if it is better to let five decision support queries run at once, or let only three run at once and let the other two wait.

The **onstat -g mgm** command allows you to see the status of decision support queries—how many are waiting, how much resource each query is using, and so on. This output and some query timings are the principal method an administrator has for tuning the PDQ parameters. It will also be used to determine why a query might be waiting to run.

Here's a sample **onstat -g mgm** report, with explanations of each section interspersed.

```
Memory Grant Manager (MGM)

-------------------------
```

This section lists the current setting of the memory grant manager configuration parameters:

```
MAX_PDQ_PRIORITY: 100

DS_MAX_QUERIES: 3

DS_MAX_SCANS: 10

DS_TOTAL_MEMORY: 3000 KB
```

This section lists the number of active queries, the number of ready queries (queries that are waiting for a resource to run, e.g., memory, scan threads, DS_MAX_QUERIES), and the total number of decision support queries that can run at one time (DS_MAX_QUERIES).

```
Queries:Active Ready Maximum
           3      0     3
```

This section lists the total amount of memory available for decision support queries (DS_TOTAL_MEMORY) and the amount of free memory.

Memory is allocated to a query in units of a quantum, which is DS_TOTAL_MEMORY/DS_MAX_QUERIES; in the example, this is $3000/3 = 1000$. This value is listed in the Quantum column. This means that 1,000 KB will be reserved for a query even if it is not used.

```
Memory: Total Free Quantum
(KB)    3000   0   1000
```

This section lists the total number of scan threads available for decision support queries (DS_MAX_SCANS) and the number of scan threads available.

Scan threads are allocated in units of a quantum, which is DS_MAX_SCANS/DS_MAX_QUERIES, which is $10/3 = 3$ (rounded down). The Quantum column lists this size. Scan threads are allocated in units of a quantum even though the quantum may not be used by one query.

```
Scans: Total Free Quantum
         10    7    3
```

This section lists the number of decision support queries that are waiting for a particular resource. The query must be granted all the necessary resources before it can run. Each resource can be thought of as a "gate": the gate cannot be entered until enough resources are available. Each "gate" the query can wait on is listed below, with the number of queries waiting for that resource.

```
Load Control:(Memory)(Scans)(Priority)(Max Queries)(Reinit)
             Gate 1 Gate 2 Gate 3   Gate 4       Gate 5
(Queue Length)0      0      0        0            0
```

The next section lists the active decision support queries. Two numbers are listed in the **Memory** and **Thread** columns: the number of scan threads currently used/granted and the amount of memory currently being used/granted. The memory is in units of 8k. The example below shows each query using 1000 kbytes of memory. Only the third query is currently scanning the table.

```
Active Queries:
---------------
```

```
Session Query Priority Thread  Memory Scans Gate
  10   c666c0 2         be62d8  125/125 0/1  -
  12   c726c0 2         bfa508  125/125 0/1  -
  11   c6c6c0 2                 125/125 1/1  --
```

This section lists any decision support queries waiting on a resource and the resource they are waiting on. The example below shows no query waiting.

```
Ready Queries: None
```

Finally, the last section shows an average of the amount of memory and scan threads that were free, as well as the average number of queries that were active at once and in the ready queue.

```
Free Resource  Average #       Minimum #
-------------  --------------  ---------
Memory         93.8 +- 119.7   0
Scans          7.5 +- 1.3      6


Queries        Average #       Maximum # Total #
-------------  --------------  --------- -------
Active         2.3 +- 1.0      3          4
Ready          1.0 +- 0.0      1          1
```

Index